Thoughts of William T. Smith

Serving The Lord Until Death Part 1 From Earth

WILLIAM T. SMITH

SERVING THE LORD UNTIL DEATH PART 1 FROM EARTH

Bennett books may be ordered through booksellers or by contacting:

Bennett Media and Marketing

1603 Capitol Ave., Suite 310 A233

Cheyenne, WY 82001

www.thebennettmediaandmarketing.com

Phone: 1-307-202-9292

ISBN

978-1-957114-75-0   (Paperback)

978-1-957114-76-7   (eBook)

My Thanks

Every thought and poem is in thanks to my Savior.
To my family and friends, who some of these poems
and thoughts are about.
A special thanks to my brother Jim, whose book
"Nuggets of Gold" ISBN 978-0-692-06545-7

A special thanks to my nephew Herbie, whose book
"Keepers of the Dawn" E-book only keeps inspiring me to write.

A special thanks to the soldiers who keeps us free.
A special thanks to the ministers who preach God's Word.
A special thanks to the doctors and nurses around the world.
A special thanks to all the volunteers.
My heart felt thanks goes out for the special work
that only you can do.
My thanks and prayers be with you all - Amen.

William T. Smith

The Dedication

I wish to dedicate this book to all my brothers and sisters:
James Jr - Marvin - Floyd - Elsie - Raymond - Herbert - Mary -
Martha - Clarence - Kenneth

A Note From the Author

I wish to thank my Lord and Savior for this book.
It was Him that laid a book on my heart.
These thoughts and poems are to honor and glorify Jesus.
I may have penned them, but: the Holy Spirit actually wrote them.
My prayer is that these thoughts and poems will somehow
inspire you to write.
When you do, let Jesus lead you with the Holy Spirit.
Thanks very much for reading this book.
My hope is that you will get one of the other books I have written.

William T. Smith

These poems and thoughts came from my life experiences:
The Holy Bible (KJV):
Things I read in newspapers:
Things I heard on TV News:
To the best of my knowledge, I have not copied from anyone.

Born Again

Have you ever wondered what the phrase "born again" means? The Bible records that Jesus used the phrase in a conversation with a man named Nicodemus. Nicodemus approached Jesus at night. He was curious about Jesus and the Kingdom of God.

Jesus told him: "Unless someone is born again, he cannot see the Kingdom of God" (John 3:3). Nicodemus responded, "But how can anyone be born when he is old"? (John 3:4).

Nicodemus was a highly moral man who obeyed God's law. He was a respected leader of the Jewish community. No doubt he was a fine man. Yet something was lacking. Like Nicodemus, many people today confuse religion with new birth in Christ. Phrases like "I believe there is a God" often are confused with a real new-birth experience.

New birth begins with the Holy Spirit convicting a person that the person is a sinner. Because of sin, we are spiritually dead. For this reason, spiritual birth, as Jesus described it, is necessary. God loves us and gives us spiritual birth when we ask Him for it.

The Bible says all persons are sinners (Romans 3:23). Jesus died on a cross and, was raised from the dead to save sinners. To be born again means that a person admits to God that he or she is a sinner, repents of sin, believes in or trust Christ, and confesses faith in Christ as Savior and Lord. Jesus told Nicodemus that everyone that believes in (places faith in) Christ would not perish (John 3:16). Jesus is the only One who can save us (John 14:6).

Jesus Christ was with God the Father before the world was created. He became human and lived among humanity as Jesus of Nazareth. He came to show us what God the Father is like. He lived a sinless life, showing us how to live; and He died upon a cross to pay for our sins. God raised Him from the dead.

Jesus is the source of eternal life. Jesus wants to be the doorway to new life for you. In the Bible He was called the "Lamb of God" (John 1:29). In the Old Testament, sacrifices were made for sins of the people. Jesus became the sacrificial lamb offered for your sin.

Jesus said, "I am the way, the truth, and the life. No one comes to the Father except through Me" (John 14:6).

He is waiting for you now.

Admit to God that you are a sinner, means to repent, or turn away from your sin.

By faith receive Jesus Christ as God's Son and accept Jesus' gift of forgiveness from sin. He took the penalty for your sin by dying on the cross.

Confess your faith in Jesus Christ as Savior and Lord.

To believe in Jesus is to be born again. Confess your sins and ask Jesus right now to save you.

"Whoever calls on the name of the Lord will be saved" (Acts 2:21).

You may say a prayer similar to this as you call on God to save you: You must do this with an honest willing heart.

"Dear God, I know that you love me. I confess my sin and need of salvation. I turn away from my sin and place my faith in Jesus as my Savior and Lord. In Jesus' name I pray, Amen".

After you have received Jesus Christ into your life, tell a pastor or another Christian you have received Jesus Christ into your life, share your decision with another person, and following Christ's example, ask for baptism by immersion in your local church as a public expression of your faith (Romans 6:4; Colossians 2:6).

EXPLORE THE BIBLE

Lifeway

Table of Contents

Pledge To The American Flag

I pledge my allegiance to the flag of the United States of America, and to the Republic for which it stands. One nation under God, indivisible, with liberty and justice for all.

Pledge To The Christian Flag

I pledge my allegiance to the Christian Flag and to the Savior for whose Kingdom it stands. One Savior, crucified, risen, and coming again with life liberty to all who believe.

Pledge To The Bible

I pledge my allegiance to the Bible, God's Holy Word, I will make it a lamp unto my feet and a light unto my path and will hide its words in my heart that I might not sin against God.

BOOK ONE

God of Israel

I have not been there, but I do love Israel.

For I know that she is God's chosen people.

Oh; Israel how I long to see the twelve tribe

Living in one country and at God's blessed side.

There are wars on every border of this country.

The Nations want peace, and have a signed treaty.

The treaty is signed; the Temple can now be built.

But: Remember Jesus is your King; your offering of sin guilt.

But I am still aware of what the Bible says about;

The way the Nation will be deceived with peace shouts.

How Judea will flee before the army of the world.

For: the Antichrist came-in and took over at a blur.

But: you Israel will be the victor as this age end.

Because: God is your leader, and with Jesus you do win.

William T. Smith

My Writings

I do these writings, not because I want to go to heaven.
I do these writings, because I want you to be there with me.
I do these writings, not because I want Jesus to save me.
I do these writings, because Jesus did save my soul from sin.

These writings are to let you know that there is a heaven.
These writings are to let you know that Jesus is real, the Son.
These writings are to let you know what the trinity is all about.
These writings are to let you know about hell, repent from sin.

I write because I love the Lord God- Jesus Christ- my Creator.
I write because I want you to love the same God that I do.
I write because I do not wish to be silent about my God's grace.
I write out of respect, not because I have to for any other reason.

William T. Smith

Our Rights

For over 200 years the Constitution has protected us.

We had freedom to speak our minds without persecution.

We had freedom to bare arms for our life and protection.

We had freedom to go and do what ever we wanted; unless:

That freedom affected someone else's freedom to live well.

It seems now that the freedom we enjoy so much in this land.

Is now in jeopardy of being a crime against the state of affairs.

Our Ministers are being censored with the message of truth.

Our income is being taxed so much, we are having problems.

Our nation is being invaded by illegals, drugs and murder.

Our teachers has to be communist, in order to be able to teach.

All of this is coming to pass for a special reason, in todays world.

That reason is that God is sending His Son back to redeem us.

The world must be in total chaos, before Jesus can do the harvest .

This is happening right before our eyes, and we are to blind to see.

Please consider our rights, and how they are disappearing fast.

Then ask God's Son Jesus to forgive you of your sin and shame.

Jesus will come into your heart and give you hope and peace.

William T. Smith

Death Angel

I was lying in bed, with the Death Angel at my side.

I asked the Death Angel if he would let me to say good bye.

The Angel said I had a little time, but make it short and sweet.

I let my children know I was going home, my supper is ready.

They looked at me like I was crazy, but did not say a word.

The table is set and ready for me to eat with my Lord Jesus.

Jesus is calling me home to be with Him in His glorious peace.

For I gave Him my heart, soul and life when I said I was sorry.

What was I sorry for: For disobeying His commandments.

When Jesus died on that tree, it was for my sin that He was sent.

So I accepted Jesus as Lord God and Savior of my soul.

Now it is supper time for me, and from this earth I must go.

I wish to see you all in this glorious heaven of Jesus with me.

But: the only way is to accept Jesus as Savior, for glory to see.

William T. Smith

Return of Jesus

I have been asked: "When do you think the Lord will return"?

My answer is: "I know not the day or hour; just the season".

As was in the time of Noah, so will it be at His (Jesus) return!

How was it in the time of Noah, they were eating and drinking.

They were marring and given in marriage, and doing as they pleased.

Homosexually was running wild, with all sorts of evil following.

Everyone doing what they wish and leaving God out of the picture.

When you look around today, the same thing is going on here.

The season and the time is getting closer and closer everyday.

According to the Bible, more things must happen before the rapture.

One: The Temple of God, in Jerusalem must be rebuilt on the mount.

Two: The Antichrist must defile this very Temple of God, of the Jews.

Three: The money will be useless, something else will take it's place.

Four: You will have to take a mark of some kind, to buy, sell or trade.

Five: There will be only one religion through out the whole world.

Six: There will be only one government through out the whole world.

Seven: There will be world peace with Israel and the Jews; seemly.

When you see all of these things happening in this world of ours.

That is when you will know the time is very short,

you should be ready.

William T. Smith

Paper Towels

I went to the store to get some toilet paper for I was out.
When I got to the shelf, no toilet paper here; I shouted.
The manager said: "The pandemic has been here a while".
But: go to the paper towels, I think I have some in that aisle.
So I went to get some paper towels, guest what, not there.
So I said: "What is this no toilet paper or paper towels either.
It looks like napkins will have to do in this here pinch I'm in.
But: the napkin aisle was empty also, here I am about to stink.
Then I picked up the paper and read it at the line by the stand.
It told about a person whose toilet and paper towel was ruined;
They had several bundles on their porch when the rain came.
The question is this: why is paper more important than groceries?
I know they cannot eat this paper when hunger hits their stomach.

William T. Smith

I'll Fly Away

There is a gospel song that we sing: I'll fly away.
It is called that, for on this earth I cannot stay.
One verse has it written what will really happen.
The Bible does proclaim that this is very sound.
When I die, Hallelujah bye and bye, I'll fly away.
This body will stay here; but not my soul and spirit.
The Word states that flesh and blood cannot enter in.
This body is corruptible seed, and cannot enter heaven.
The kingdom of God are for those who accept the Son.
For Jesus is Lord and the Savior of our soul on earth.
If you cannot accept Jesus as your Savior and Lord.
You are serving Satan,and will be in hell for sure.

William T. Smith

Tree of Life

Jesus is a tree of life, flowing out from me.

I accepted Him as my Savior, for everyone to see.

Jesus is the root; with me being only one branch.

I need to be pruned, and every now and then lanced.

This is done so I can glorify Jesus, my God and Savior.

Sin entered into this world, I was separated from God.

But Jesus loved me, that is why He sent His Son Jesus.

Jesus who knew no sin, took my sin and died on the cross.

Jesus did not stay in the grave, He rose the third day.

He was punished for the sin I did, so I may live.

Now with my life, I want others to have this life also.

So I tell them about Jesus and the saving grace of God.

William T. Smith

A New Body

Everyone that was ever born at death will receive a new body.

For this earthly body will go back to dust from where it came.

After death we will not need this body to be our temple anymore.

We will have an eternal body, so we will be able to face the Holy God.

From the sweat of your face shall you eat bread,

until you return to the ground.

For out of the ground you were formed,

unto the ground you shall return.

Abraham spoke to God and said: I am nothing but dust and ashes.

The people I have created, shall praise the Lord God on earth.

We will be absent from this body, and present with the Lord, if we:

Accept Christ as Lord and your body becomes the temple of the Lord.

The Lord says that we will all be changed into an incorruptible body.

Those who do not accept, will be changed,

but corruptible cannot inherit glory.

Accept Jesus today and at your death you will live forever more.

Do not accept Jesus and at your death you will die forever more.

William T. Smith

My Redeemer Lives

Jesus is my redeemer, He gave His earthly life for me.

But: He did not stay in the grave, He arose for all to see.

He was witness by over 500 people, yes my redeemer lives.

He lives in my heart, and is an advocate unto the Father.

I know this without a doubt, that my redeemer lives.

My hope is; that you also know that your redeemer lives.

What is a redeemer, and how do we really know he's true?

A redeemer is a person that restores someone back as new.

He took my hateful heart and turned it into a loving heart.

I know my redeemer lives, because He helps me in this life.

For nobody can come to the Father unless it is through Jesus.

And one day I will see Him face to face before the Father.

William T. Smith

Faith

What is faith? A result from a impossible hopeful situation.

Without faith, what you hope for may not come to pass.

But: faith alone can do nothing, unless you act upon it.

So faith without works cannot produce any tangible action.

If you wish to get results with faith; you must have hope.

Hope is what will cause your faith to become very strong.

How may you ask? When you have hope, you must have faith.

So hope and faith goes hand in hand with work, for it to pass.

But: true results comes, only if you have love; Love conquers all.

Love is what activates both faith and hope; this heavenly love.

If you have love, then your faith and hope is not being selfish.

When you are asking for something, please do not ask amiss.

In other words; do not ask for selfish,worldly, evil things.

Ask for something that will or may help someone else be better.

William T. Smith.

Debauchery

What is debauchery; and how is it related to God Almighty?

This is what the dictionary says about the word debauchery.

Extreme indulgence in sensuality or orgies or archaic.

Or a seduction from virtue or duty; or to lead away from excellence.

I decided to look in the dictionary for some of these definitions.

The dictionary for the word sensuality has: deficient in morals,

spiritual, or intellectual interests; devoted to or preoccupied with self.

The dictionary for the word orgy has: an excessive sexual indulgence.

The dictionary for the word archaic has: of, relating to, or characteristic

of an earlier or more primitive time; something resembling the truth.

God gave these people over to uncleanness of their lust Romans 1:24.

Now I understand why Romans 1:24 was written; God cannot stand sin.

Also the fact that this also dishonors the body as well as the mind.

So God had to give them over to an reprobate mind of uncleanness.

The Bible says: For there is no respect of persons with God Romans 2:11.

Who will render to every man and woman according to their deeds.

If you disrespect what the Bible says about the way you are living.

Then God will let you go ahead and live the way that you choose to live.

Remember this: You will always reap what you are sowing in this life.

You will die in your sin and be punished through out eternity in hell.

William T. Smith

BOOK TWO

We Are Different

Every creature on earth is marvelous in their own way.
For God the Creator has created all of us; as the Bible says.
Red, yellow, black or white; makes no different dark or light.
We have all been created for a purpose, precious in His sight.
We are very different from each other; but: we are unique.
In the way we live, act, work and even in the way we think.
Our culture, our politics, our schools and even our religion.
All these things are different; as we compare and we see them.
Our DNA, what holds us together; as well as our fingerprints.
These are very different from one person to another person.
But: take a closer look, we are still all the same in what we do.
Yes: everything is all about me, only me; nothing about you.
But you see; we all need salvation that comes through Christ.
The sin that we commit started at birth, and will not last.
Jesus is God in the flesh; who came to forgive our sin on earth.
So remember: we are wonderfully made for God, starting at birth.
Each one of us looks and acts the same; we all have sinned.
Each one of us needs a savior, that can forgive and forget differences.

William T. Smith

What Matters

We hear a lot on what matters in the world.
Black lives says that they matter over the white.
The white says that they are being discriminated.
Abortionist say a child's life does not matter.
The Church preaches that all life does matters.
Our leaders keep telling us, all things matter.
All of this is absolutely true in one way or another.
Everything that goes on in this world matters to God.
For Creator God, created this world for the human race.
But the most important thing that matters is Jesus Christ.
For God so loved this world that He gave His Son for it.
Not to condemn the world, But to save the people in it.
So that we may have communication with Jesus the Son.
All life matters to God in the fact that God wants all life.
So God sent His Son to die on a cross for our sinful ways.
Jesus also rose on the third day, to give us eternal life.
Now we can taste salvation from God, and peace it gives.
In fact: the only thing that really matters is the love of God.
It was God's love for us that Jesus died and rose from the dead.
That way, whosoever says yes to Jesus, will have eternal life.
Being Jesus rose from the dead, so shall we also rise from death.
What really matters? Life matters with Jesus, God's only Son.
The only way; is to accept Jesus as your Lord, God and Savior.

William T. Smith

Work for Salvation

I did not have to work, for God to forgive my sin.

I did not have to work, for God to give me salvation.

All I had to do was believe, Jesus is God the Christ.

God came to earth as a human, died for all my sin.

What I had to do was believe Jesus is the Messiah.

He did not stay in the grave, but arose for my salvation.

Jesus was whipped beyond recognition for my healing.

Jesus carried a cross up a hill and died, so I can be free.

But: Jesus did not stay in that grave after he was buried.

Jesus arose so when I believe, He gave me the Holy Spirit.

Jesus is God in the flesh, lived and died for the world.

Heavenly Father is God in heaven, who watches and judges.

Holy Spirit is God in the spirit, who leads and guides us.

All three is Creator God, and you cannot separate them.

I work; not to receive salvation or forgiveness of my sin.

I work for crowns that, so I can lay them at Jesus' feet.

Salvation comes the moment I believe that Jesus is God.

Crowns come when I do things pleasing to Jesus; my God.

William T. Smith

The Reason I Sing

The reason I sing and the reason I do shout.
Jesus saved my soul and kicked the Devil out.
Thank You Lord; for saving my sin filled soul.
Thank You Lord; for everything that I know.
Thank You Lord; for always being there for me.
Thank You Lord; for letting me become your heir.

The reason I sing and the reason I do shout.
Jesus saved my soul and kicked the Devil out.
Thank You Lord; for the Bible that I read about you.
Thank You Lord; for the insights within the pages.
Thank You Lord; for making salvation so clear.
Thank You Lord; for bringing glory down to me.

The reason I sing and the reason I do shout.
Jesus saved my soul and kicked the Devil out.
Thank You Lord; for the Holy Spirit in me to live.
Thank You Lord; for his guiding power and light.
Thank You Lord; for letting him be my comforter.
Thank You Lord; for giving me grace, joy and peace.

The reason I sing and the reason I do shout.
Jesus saved my soul and kicked the Devil out.

William T. Smith

Not Afraid

I am not afraid of getting the COVID-19 virus.

I am not afraid if I die from this COVID-19.

I know where I will be after sickness and die.

For I will be in glory with Jesus at my side.

I will not temp the Lord my God, by being stupid.

I will wear a mask, while in stores and around people.

I will not temp the Lord my God, with my doings.

Not because I am afraid, but: I want His protection.

With or without the protection of the Lord Jesus Christ.

I may get this Covid-19, and I may surely die from it.

But: if I do get it and I die from complications from it.

I will praise Jesus, for keeping me from something worse.

William T. Smith

Do We Care?

Should we care about what is going on in the world today?

Have we forgot what Islam done to the world and country?

Should we let Islam destroy Pakistan and world like they want?

Remember they also wanted to destroy the USA's government!

If we let Islam have their way; they will never stop harming.

Every country in the world will be at their merciless killings.

We know from the pass as well as what is happing right now.

Islam has no mercy on anyone but Islam, not even the Muslim.

President Biden may not care what happens in the world of Pakistan.

But: as a world leader he should, for what is happening will not stop.

President Biden has already proved that he does not care about USA.

So I feel he will still not care what happens in the world either.

After all, isn't he letting Vice-President Harris do most of his work.

William T. Smith

Understand

We believe in many things, that we do not understand.
Like when we plant a seed in the ground, it will grow.
We may not know how this happens, but we still plant.
What we get is the produce of that seed, with the plant.

We believe that we need oxygen, water and food to live.
We may not understand how all this works in our body.
But: we do know without these elements, we cannot live.
So we believe, without knowledge of how it all works.

The same goes with the trinity; Father, Son and Holy Spirit.
Understanding this is very difficult; believing is not hard.
We believe in what we cannot see, or know, or understand.
But by faith we know it all works, the way it is suppose to.

We have enough faith to believe what we do not understand.
Then we should believe there is a God who loves us more.
Loved us enough to send His Son (Jesus) to die in our place.
So that when we die physically, we will live forever eternally.

William T. Smith

Everlasting Life

What is this thing called everlasting life or eternal life?
The definition for this seems to be sharper than a knife.
How can a person live forever, when there is death all around?
This I have to ponder and see if a good answer can be found.
If you forsake houses, family, land or even your spouse;
And follow Jesus, you shall inherit this everlasting life.
If you feed the hungry, and give water to the thirsty, or
Cloth the naked and visit prisoners, you will have eternal life.
If you believe in Jesus, ask to be forgiven, you will have eternal life.
This is the true God, The Son, Jesus Christ is everlasting life.
The righteousness of God came in the form of Jesus Christ.
Even though he died, he will live forever more in heaven- glory.
Yes Jesus died for your sin, he arose from the grave for your soul.
Jesus is alive, and living in the hearts of all who believes he is God.

William T. Smith

The Perfect Birthday Gift

People all around the world gives very good birthday gifts.

There are many gifts that seem to be perfect for someone.

One person may receive a new automobile that they wanted.

While another may get a vacation of a life time somewhere.

I have heard of getting a house or a peace of land, as a gift.

Or maybe an animal that the person likes to have in their life.

All these gifts are good and many may seem to be perfect.

But: my brother received a gift that no one could ever beat.

My brother Kenny lived a life for his savior; Jesus Christ.

And the birthday gift he received on his 73rd year was this.

He went to bed the night before his birthday, with gospel music.

He never woke-up on the earth; but passed on into eternity.

Kenny woke-upon his 73rd birthday in the arms of Christ Jesus.

What a perfect birthday gift that had to be, waking up in glory.

Kenny went peacefully that night into eternity of God almighty.

He is now rejoicing with all his kinfolk who believed in Jesus.

Now: if that is not a perfect gift, then what would you call it.

Yes: Kenny gave his heart and life to Jesus for all to know and see.

One day I also will be there, rejoicing with my brothers and sisters.

The ones that accepted Jesus as their Lord and Savior and King.

William T. Smith

God

In the beginning God created Heaven and Earth.
Before anything that is, there was a God at first.
In Genesis God is called a Creator who is creating.
He is also called Eternal, Omnipotent and Holy.
God said: Let us make man in our image and likeness.
So God created man in His image, but not in likeness.
We are created in three parts, just like our Creator God.
God the Father; God the Son; and God the Holy Spirit.

Like God man has three parts also; Heart, Soul and Spirit.
The heart of man is his personality or some call attitude.
The heart of God is the same, We call him Son or Lord.
The soul of man is his character or what some call nature.
The soul of God is the same, We call him Father or I Am.
The spirit of man is his morals, conscience, or ethics.
The spirit of God is the same, We call him the Holy Spirit.
All three makes of what man or God is; there is no separation.

We do not worship three Gods, but one God (God the Creator).
We do not acknowledge three persons, but one person (human).
If you want to know about God, read His Word- the Holy Bible.
If you want to know about man, look at what he is writing.

William T. Smith

A Story to Tell

Come on in, coffee is hot and sit for a spell.

I have a good story, and for you I must tell.

It's about a boy that was born at midnight.

In a barn that was dirty, but: what a sight.

This boy grow and was two years of age.

The King in the land wanted him very dead.

The parents escaped on that frightful night.

Moved to another country, to escape the fight.

The boy grew into a man of mighty bliss.

The Devil who wished him dead, put him to a test.

The boy, now a man, withstood those tests for him.

He went out to preach the Word to all that listened.

The man was 33 years old, when it finally happened.

The Devil finally put him on a cross to kill him.

This man did die on that cross, and he was buried.

But: on the third day he rose from that grave and death.

The man's name was Jesus, Son of the living God.

Jesus went through this as punishment for mans sin.

Believe in Jesus as Son of God- Messiah- and Christ.

You will have life eternal with him in his heaven.

Reject Jesus as your Savior- Redeemer- King- and Lord.

Spend your eternity in torment separated from Gods love.

William T. Smith

My House

I bought a house, lived there for many years.
It is now old, and in need of a lot of repairs.
I bought a new house, better in so many ways.
No wish to go back to my old house, on any day.
This body that I am living in, while on earth.
Is my temple or house I received at my birth.
I have not taken very good care of this temple.
It aches with many pains, and will not stay still.
One day I will trade this house for a brand new one.
The Word says; when I die, this house I will shun.
I will receive a new house, that is eternal and whole.
So: why would I want to come back to this home?
My old house is this earthly temple I am living in.
My new house is my eternal temple after this life.
Where you will be with this new temple is up to you.
Accept Jesus as Savior and Lord, you will be in glory.
Reject Jesus as Savior and Lord, and end-up in hell.

William T. Smith

BOOK THREE

The Harvest

As I look at the fields of brown corn and beans.

I know that the harvest is just about to begin.

The crops all summer long was very green and tall.

The growing season is about four months long.

When Jesus said the fields are ripe for the harvest.

He was talking about the souls of people spiritually.

When you look at the earth today, it is still ready.

People wants to listen to preachers with a message.

The message is this, do what you want it is Okay.

The message they need to hear is, repent of your sin.

But: you may look at this harvest in a different light.

Satan has people going to and fro, doing evil things.

Jesus said it would be that way at the end times.

Look closely at the harvest, are you ready for it?

William T. Smith

I Worship a Working God

There are three parts to our Creator, Omnipotent God.

The three parts are His personality, morals and character.

These same three parts are in every human, or mankind.

When you remove one part, the other two cannot work.

When you worship your god; is he complete, is he one?

The God I worship is Heavenly Father, Lord Jesus, Holy Spirit.

These three makes up one God; Creator, Omnipotent, Eternal.

He is a working God in the creation that only He could create.

If you would like to serve this living, working eternal God?

All you have to do is believe, believe on His Son (Christ Jesus).

Jesus is the heart of God; Or God's personality or Attitude.

The Holy Spirit is the morals of God; God's conduct or belief.

The Heavenly Father is the nature of God; God's character or mind.

When you put the three together, you are worshiping a Holy God.

A God that created the heaven, earth and the heavens above earth.

A God that created man, and will work in your life, if you let Him.

William T. Smith

Do You Know The Day and Hour?

I woke-up this morning with a lot of plans for the day.
I was full of energy, my outlook bright, now a ditch I lay.
Knowing not if I will live or die, will I ever get back home?
When you are lying in a ditch, not able to move and alone.
Many thoughts will come to your mind, will I live or die?
Where will I be if I die and stand before my maker in eternity?
Jesus said: "That we know not the day or hour of death".
When we do die, what happens to what we hold so dear?
As I lie here, I suddenly realized that was not a concern I have.
My concern is, Where am I going to spend eternity for all time?
Did I live my life just for myself, family, work, and not for God?
Will I hear the words of Jesus saying: "Welcome home my son"?
Or: will I hear the statement: "Depart from me, you doer of evil"?
Do I have time enough to give my heart to the Lord, before I die?
I have waited until the last moment; will I make it into heaven?
Don't be like me and wait; for in waiting you may not have the time.

William T. Smith

His Image

God said: "Let us make man in Our image, after Our likeness".

The reason God said Our is because He was reasoning with Himself.

God created man in His own image, male and female created them.

Notice God created man in His image, but: not inHis likeness.

If God created man in His likeness, we would be like Him; sinless.

We would be worshiping God by His nature, not by faith believing.

God did not want to have robots worshiping Him without faith.

So God created man in His image, but: not in His likeness.

That way we as humans; "male and female" have a choice to make.

We can serve God through His Son "Jesus", or go our own way.

If we choose Jesus, we will be in His likeness for all eternity.

If we choose our own way, we will be forever in darkness of His light.

William T. Smith

Will You be Ready?

When Judgment comes knocking at your death door.
Will you be ready to meet God, your creator?
God loves you so much, that He sent His Son for you.
Jesus is the Son, and He died on a cross for your sin.
If you answered my question with a "Yes I am".
Then you have accepted Jesus as your Lord and Savior.
When you meet the judgment, you will hear this:
"Welcome home thou true and faithful servant of Jesus".
If you answered my question with a "No I am not":
Then you have not accepted Jesus ' and living for yourself.
When you meet the judgment, you will hear this:
"Depart from me you doer of sin, I know you not".
If you are not sure if you are ready, and have some doubts.
Probably you are not, if you knew, you would have peace.
Accepting Jesus as your Lord and Savior, is asking forgiveness.
Come as you are and ask; then the repentance starts in your soul.

William T. Smith

Wisdom

The Bible asked a question: Where can wisdom be found?
If you look in the open spaces you will hear wisdom calling.
For you see, wisdom cannot be silent, it has to call out load.
Only wisdom can discover what is far off, or what is profound.
Wisdom is where the understanding will dwell in your heart.
Where no mortal comprehend what wisdom really is worth.
For you see; wisdom is more precious than diamonds or gold.
As you look for pearls, look for wisdom and understanding.
Kingdom of God is like a hidden treasure, find it you find wisdom.
Sell your soul to the Lord, and find his wisdom and understanding.
Wisdom cannot be found in the land of the living, only in God:
Because wisdom and understanding belongs to God the giver.

Job asked the question: Where then does wisdom come from?
Job then asked the second question: Where does understanding dwell?
For God alone knows where both comes from and where they dwell.
God alone understands all the ways of wisdom and it will be used?
Wisdom dwells together with prudence in Jesus our Lord and God.
To reverence the Lord is wisdom; but: destruction is of the evil one.
To reverence is to have wisdom; to disobey causes many destructions.
Reverence of the Lord, is the beginning of wisdom and understanding.
If you are wise in understanding, your wisdom rewards you.
You can always find wisdom on the lips of the discerning person.
In wisdom you store up hope, understanding and knowledge.

The wisdom of the Lord views the ends of the earth, with understanding.
The wisdom of the Lord sees everything under the heavens of earth.

When God looks at wisdom, He always will praise and glorify it.
The Lord will confirm wisdom and He will test this same wisdom.
When you reverence the Lord - you will know it is His wisdom.
Always shun evil and you will understand the wisdom of the Lord.
Does not the understanding of wisdom raise her voice in knowledge?
Does not the knowledge of wisdom arise in your writing of understanding?

William T. Smith

Jesus' Tomb

When I die and put in the ground.
After a while, I will be nothing but dust.
This happens to everyone that is born.
No matter if child of God or a evil doer.
But when Jesus was put into that tomb.
There was no dust, nor was any bones;
There is a good reason for this to be so.
For Jesus was all human as well as all God.
The only person that is in the heavenly ream;
Will be Jesus, for His body could not stay;
Jesus is all God, therefore he can not be dust.
The dust would show that Jesus was not God.
Jesus is God in the flesh, so there is no bones.
Jesus is God in the spirit, so there is no dust.
No dust, no bones, no body is to be found.
Jesus was not a mere man; He is a Holy God.

William T. Smith

Death Bed

Here I lay on this hard cold death bed.
Given my last meal on earth, I am fed.
When I close my eyes to sleep to night.
I know I will be carried home into glory.
I will have a new body in God's eternity.
With no pain, no sorrows in a celestial body.
I will be with Jesus my Lord, and my Savior.
I will stay with Jesus my God forever.
You can also have this confidence at death.
Give your soul and life over to Christ Jesus.
All you need to do is ask and believe.
Ask for forgiveness of sin and wrong doings.
Believe Jesus is God in the flesh; and in spirit.

William T. Smith

Thanksgiving

Thanksgiving is here, and a dinner is cooked.
I am with some family members, but not all.
I am the last of eleven children, that was born.
With one sister and five brothers already dead.
My nephews and nieces all have their gathering.
So we all cannot be together for thanksgiving.
I am thankful for those I still have and can visit.
I pray that I will be here next thanksgiving day.
But if not, I know I will be with my new family.
Jesus has a table spread with everybody near.
I will be happy and joyful with all the saints.
Because Jesus will be there as brother and Father.

William T. Smith

Your Vision

Do you have a vision for your life to live?
What kind of plans are you making today?
What is your life goal in the work force?
What is your goal in the world of finance?
Do you desire a big house, out in the country?
Do you just want an apartment in the city?
Do you desire to be a successful business man?
Do you just want to work and play with family?
No matter what you desire , or your vision is.
Never leave out God in your plans and dreams.
Without God, your desires, visions is never enough.
Put God into your life, by accepting Jesus His Son.
Your desires, and plans should be basted on above.
With Jesus in your corner, your vision may change.
Without Jesus your vision will be nothing but a vision.
You may gain the whole world, and loss your soul.
What have you gained in doing all this work?
You will have nothing but torment in your life and soul.

William T. Smith

My Rest

Jesus is my hope, and in Him I do rest.

The Spirit of Jesus lets me do my best.

When Satan comes at me with temptations.

I give it to Jesus, He takes it without a fuss.

Jesus said to put my burdens on his shoulder.

When I do, then I can rest in His grace.

It is the grace of God that keeps me going.

What I cannot do, Jesus has already done.

William T. Smith

Tribulation

Here I sit in my big chair, in my elaborate office.
Thinking about my fortune, with plenty to eat.
I have a garage full of antic automobiles and bikes.
Thinking I have it made, with all the things I like.
I never thought I could lose it all, every single peace.
But: the economy went sour, and I lost it all; everything.
Now I am begging from the people that I was boss over.
They say that I should have invested my money better.
I don't know what happened, I lost everything this year.
The virus was bad, and my investments was lost.
Now: I got a truck load of money, that is worthless.
I cannot buy anything, nor can I sell or trade my stuff.
We have a one bank system that knows the wealth.
We have a one world religion with no respect at all.
We have a one health group that will not pay at all.
We have a one world politics that govern very badly.
I cannot speck out, for the spies are every where.
They will come at you with burdens I cannot bare.
I know not what I should do, or where I should go.
For only those with the Mark are living in luxury now.

William T. Smith

How To Become a Christian

By taking three steps, you can make the most important decision of your life—to accept Jesus as your personal Savior and Lord and His gift of forgiveness of your sins.

Admit

Admit to God that you are a sinner. Repent, turn away from your sin: For all have sinned, and come short of the glory of God; Romans 3:23. For the wages of sin is death; but the gift of God is eternal life through Jesus Christ our Lord. Romans 6:23. Repent you therefore, and be converted, that your sins may be blotted out, when the times of refreshing shall come from the presents of the Lord; Acts 3:19.

Believe

By faith receive Jesus Christ as God's Son and accept Jesus' gift of forgiveness from sin. For God so loved the world, that he gave his only begotten Son, that whosoever believes in him should not perish, but have everlasting life. John 3:16. Jesus said unto him, I am the way, the truth,, and the life; no man comes unto the Father, but by me. John 14;6. Neither is there salvation in any other: for there is none other name under heaven given among men, whereby we must be saved. Acts 4:12. But God commended his love toward us, in that, while we were yet sinners, Christ died for us. Romans 5:8. For by grace are you saved through faith; and that not of yourselves: it is the gift of God: Not of works, lest any man should boast. Ephesians 2:8-9. He came unto his own, and his own received him not. But as many as received him, to them gave he power to become the sons of God, even to them that believe on his name: Which were born, not of blood, nor of the will of the flesh, nor of the will of man, but of God. John 1:11-13.

Confess

Confess your faith in Jesus Christ as Savior and Lord. If we confess our sins, he is faithful and just to forgive us our sins, and to cleanse us from all unrighteousness. I John 1:9. That if you shall confess with your mouth the Lord Jesus, and shall believe in your heart that God has raised him from the dead, you shall be saved. For with the heart man believes unto righteousness; and with the mouth confession is made unto salvation. For whosoever shall call upon the name of the Lord shall be saved. Romans 10:9-10&13.

If you choose right now to believe Jesus died for your sins and receive new life through Him, pray a prayer similar to the one that follows, as you call on Him, and Him alone, to be your Savior and Lord: But pray with an honest heart believing Jesus is your Savior, for He knows if you are sincere or not.

"Dear Heavenly Father, I know I am a sinner and have rebelled against You in many ways. I believe Jesus died for my sin and that only through faith in His death and resurrection can I be forgiven. I now turn from my sin and ask Jesus to come into my life as my Savior and Lord. From this day forward, I will choose to follow Jesus. Thank You, Lord Jesus for loving me and forgiving me. In Jesus' name I pray. Amen."

After you have received Jesus Christ into your life, share your decision with another person. Following Christ's example, ask for baptism by immersion in your local church as a public expression of your faith. Therefore we are buried with him by baptism into death: that like as Christ was raised up from the dead by the glory of the Father, even so we also should walk in newness of life. Romans 6:4.

As you have therefore received Christ Jesus the Lord, so walk you in him: Colossians 2:6.

BOOK FOUR

Courtney

Courtney: I hope you will have a good birthday.
I wanted to get you something, but did not know;
What to get a sixteen year old girl these days.
So I said to myself, "all girls really likes dolls".
Dolls are for younger girls, not a sixteen year old.
So: I thought about a dress to wear and show off.
I was told that girls do not like dresses now a days.
The dress will hang in the closet until thrown away.
So what would you get a sixteen year old girl?
There is no other thing a girl would want me to bring.
So: here you are, a brand new automobile to drive.
But: What kind would you want? What do you like?
I did not know, so: I thought I would let you choose.
So here it is; Which one do you choose? No give backs.
For a hot wheel is a hot wheel, for only you to play with.
I do not need them, so here they are and here they stay.

William T. Smith

Number Seven

The number seven shows up a lot in the Bible.
Lets start with the creation story; seven days total.
There were six of the creation;one day to rest in.
Joseph interpretation of the Pharaoh's two dreams.
One dream was about seven skinny cows, eating fat ones.
Second dream was about seven bad ears of corn ;
eating seven healthy ears of corn; that bothered the Pharaoh.
The interpretation was seven years of plenty followed;
by seven years of famine through the whole country.
Moses led the children of Israel out of bondage of Egypt.
God told Moses to prepare seven feasts to honor God.
Joshua went to Jericho, a fortified foreign city to take.
God said to march around Jericho with load singing.
This was done for six days, but on the seventh day,
March around the city seven times, and the walls fell.
Elijah told King Ahab, that it would not rain in the land;
Elijah prayed for rain seven times before he saw a cloud.
A Nobleman came to Israel to be healed of leprosy.
He was told to dip in the Jordan river seven times for healing.
King David was a man after God's own heart;
He praised God seven times everyday without fail.
Seven is a precious number in God's Holy Book, the Bible.

William T. Smith

Public Reading

I know that this is very hard to do.
Get up here to speck to all of you.
So I put together this little booklet.
In hopes that it will help you speak.
It was given to me many years ago.
Now I would like for you all to know.
Speaking in front of people is easy.
It need not to be hard, for you to read.
You are speaking what you wrote.
Or: something of importance of sorts.
Enjoy what is written upon your heart.
Never let it go away, just do your part.
When everything is done, and it is time.
To pack up your writing to go home.
I know you will come back to read.
Your speaking what you have wrote.
That is progress, and more than reading.
This is showing the Public you care.

William T. Smith

Voting in the USA

A citizen is one born in the United States of America.
A citizen is also one being naturalized to the USA.
This is found in Amendment 14- Citizenship Rights.
A citizen can vote in every and all elections held.
A citizen can vote without being abridged; deprived.
A citizen will not be prevented from voting his conscience.
On account of race, color or previous servitude; bondage.
This is found in Amendment 15- Race No Bar To Vote.
A citizen can vote, no matter the sex, male or female.
This is found in Amendment 19- Women's Suffrage.
A citizen can legally vote at the age of eighteen.
This is found in Amendment 26- Voting Age Set to 18 Years.
You cannot vote if you are in the country illegally.
You cannot vote if you are deceased, dead in the grave.
You cannot vote if you are under the age of eighteen.
You cannot vote more than one time in any election held.

William T. Smith

A Dark Day

It was very dark; worse than if it were midnight.
Dark clouds filled the sky; blocked all the sunlight.
The earth was shaking, and opening the ground.
The whole world was trembling, my heart pounding.
Why was all this happening, at this peculiar time.
A man called Jesus,whose life was hanging in the line.
He lived a good life and helped many people all around.
He was tried for a crime not his, no witness was found.
He died on that tree, went into torment, for my sin.
He freed those who believed, for death could not hold him.
Jesus is ALIVE and well, living in the hearts of Christians.
This is not where the story ends, Jesus is coming back again.
Jesus will come to take all the believers out of this world.
The unbelievers will take their earthly punishment that day.

William T. Smith

Have Mercy

Oh Lord: Please Jesus have mercy on me.
I know I don't deserve any; but: I am in sin.
I need your mercy, so I can live in peace.
For the sin I have, it needs to very much seize.
I cannot promise that I will do everything right.
Have mercy on me Lord, let me live in your sight.
I will try my best to live right; but: with your help.
I tried on my own, and I know I cannot by myself.
What I guess I am asking is, for your salvation?
Because my heart of sin, is full of faulty vitiation.
I do not deserve your love, or your peace in my life.
But Lord: I come to you hoping I can lift you on high.
I cannot promise that I will do nothing that is wrong.
But: my hope is that you will give me a place to belong.
So LORD: would you please have a little mercy on me.
I know you can give me life; and forgive my sin.
I will work for you the best I can, while here on earth.
But you will have to be with me, for Satan will lurk.
Please: let me praise the name of the Lord all my days.
I will do my best to please you in all of my earthly ways.
Thank you Lord for this peace, you have put in my heart.
I wish to serve the Lord, until death part I from this earth.

William T. Smith

Mercy Seat

There is a seat on the right side of the Heavenly Father.

Only one person can sit there-on , and no other.

The seat is called; "Mercy Seat of God" where Jesus sits.

For Jesus knew what each of us has done, and what we think.

Because of these wrong things that we do in this life.

We deserve to be in hell; separated from God- be in strife.

But Jesus said; He will go to earth as an advocate for us.

That who-so-ever believed in Jesus, will no longer be dead.

I will have mercy on that person before My Heavenly Father.

And will make them heirs to My throne as My brother.

Therefore all who accepts Jesus as their Savior, will be in glory.

All you need to do is ask for forgiveness, and be truly sorry.

The dead that is in Christ, will be with Jesus, fully resurrected.

When you were separated from Jesus, you were dead in spirit.

Jesus said we are dead, without hope, following the world.

When we say "Yes" to Jesus, we are raised into a new life.

William T. Smith

I Am Fearfully Made

"I am fearfully and wonderfully made" Psalms 119.

This statement through out the Bible it is said.

God is our Creator and He has made it all; everything;

Including all the birds and even the way they do sing;

All the land, hills and valleys, and every precious stone;

To the Lord, the whole universe, only to Him it belongs.

Yes: the Lord has fearfully and wonderfully created it all;

The creatures in every form; from the foundation was laid;

All the animals, birds and fish, from the big to the small;

All humans, red, white, black, yellow, the little and the tall;

He gave life to everything that He made here, on this earth;

Humans, animals, the rocks, the ground, with all the curves.

Everything God made, has His Light or Life established in it;

God gave humans free will, so we can choose where we sit;

If it is for what is right, or will it be for what is wrong;

We do have the say over what we want to believe and do;

We also have the say to who our master is: Jesus or Satan;

Serve God for eternal life, or reject Him for eternal death;

Yes: we are fearfully and wonderfully made in His likeness;

Jesus died on a cross, so that all mankind can have life;

The choice is up to each of us that live on this planet earth;

Continue in the earthly sin, or be born again with spiritual birth.

William T. Smith

Number Seven in Revelation

To John; to the seven churches in Asia: Revelation 1:4.

And being turned, I saw seven golden candlesticks: 1:7.

And he had in his right hand seven stars: Revelation 1:16.

And there were seven lamps of fire burning: Revelation 4:5.

Which are the seven Spirits of God Almighty: Revelation 4:5.

A book written within, sealed with seven seals: Revelation 5:1.

To seven Angels were given seven trumpets: Revelation 8:2.

Seal up those things which the seven Thunders uttered: 10:4.

Seven Angels having the seven last plagues: Revelation 15:1.

Seven golden vials full of the wrath of God: Revelation 15:7.

And there are seven kings: five fallen, one is, one to come: 17:10.

These eleven seven's are world wide, no one is exempt, no one.

Do not let these seven's scare you from reading Revelation;

But: rejoice in the Lord who saved you from these seven's;

If you accepted Jesus as Lord, Savior, King you will see some.

If not you will see the last seven's; the vials of God's wrath.

Do not be deceived; read Revelation for yourself and be informed.

Jesus is on the throne; He will cover you with His blood;

All you must do is come- come as you are and ask for forgiveness.

Forgiveness with an honest heart, believing Jesus is God's Son.

William T. Smith

Don't Listen

Satan is on my shoulder, talking in my ear.
Saying that I need to celebrate this new Year.
I know that Satan is a thief and a big lier.
How can I keep going on, while in despair?
The god of this world I realize is very sneaky.
He has been around before Adam and Eve.
He knows all the ways of the human heart.
Wants me to serve him, under key and lock.
I wish to serve my God; Jesus, God Creator.
Who gave me life at birth; and again as Savior.
Jesus died that day on a cross at Mount Calvary.
So that I and you can live with Him in eternity.

William T. Smith

Satan is a Thief

Lucifer Archangel of the Holy God Supreme.
Was a lier from the beginning of earthly time.
He even lied and deceived Adam and Eve.
And: caused them to leave the garden of Eden.
Satan is a thief, a lier and also a big coward.
When you accept Jesus, He will let you soar.
Jesus is the love we have, when we fellowship.
God wants to have fellowship with all His children.
Lucifer, Devil, Satan the three is one and the same.
A lier, a thief, a deceiver and a very big coward.
Stay with Satan and his torment will also be yours.
Jesus is the love and peace you receive with salvation.
Jesus, Father and Holy Spirit; the three is one and same.
Stay with Jesus and eternal life you will obtain in heaven.

William T. Smith

Thankful or Resentment

When you look toward Christ Jesus of Nazareth?
Do you see him as your savior or just a prophet?
If you look at Jesus as Savior, you are grateful!
If you look at Jesus as a prophet, you are resentful!
When you look at Jesus as Savior of your soul.
Then you are thankful for His death on the cross.
If you look at Jesus as prophet, you don't believe God.
You will complain, put Him down or degrade Him.
You will never see Jesus as God, in this resentful way.
Only when you see Jesus as God, you will seek salvation.
You will always be thankful for what Jesus has done.
Be it in your life, or the life of someone else you know.
Being thankful; means you do care about the soul of others.
Being thankful; means you do enjoy what's been given you.
Being thankful; means that you want to be godly like Jesus.
Being thankful; means you are trying to do your best .

William T. Smith

BOOK FIVE

Jesus is the One

There is a Hymn that most churches have sung.

Jesus is the one, yes Jesus is the only one.

When you ask: How can Jesus be the only one?

You should hear this: Because Jesus is God's Son.

God became a human, in order to bring salvation.

Jesus is that human, he died on a cross for our sin.

Jesus said in the Bible, that He is the door to heaven.

The door into His kingdom, into heavens glory.

Jesus also said, He is the way, the truth and the life.

You know the way into heaven; Jesus is that way.

You know the truth about Jesus being God's Son.

You have life, eternal life, when you accept Jesus.

Yes; Jesus is the one, the only one to receive salvation.

The only one that is God in three persons; the trinity.

When you see Jesus you see the Father. John 14: 7-10.

Keep Jesus' commandments; as He keep His Fathers.

God is a Spirit; worship him in spirit and truth. John 4:24.

Lord is that Spirit; where the spirit is there is liberty. II Cor. 3:17.

William T. Smith

Autumn 2021

The beauty of Autumn and the turning color of leaves.
Are now going quickly into winter, with the festivals.
The trees have turned and leaves falling, to make bare.
Just like the fields with the crops, all being gathered.
Things are not much different now, like the year 2020.
Wear mask in school, but elsewhere they are not needed.
Most farmers are getting their crops out fairly early.
And the ground is getting soft, with an abundance of rain.
We had pumpkins in abundance, as we put in the yard.
With a bale of straw and corn stocks with ears of corn.
With Thanksgiving around the corner, and it is still warm.
Not looking toward winter, with all the snowstorms.

William T. Smith

Heir

An heir is a person who is entitled to an inheritance.
Or: someone who succeeds in rank, title, or office.
An heir is no different from a servant when a child;
Even though he is lord of all; Galatians 4:1.
The heir has tutors and governors, as they grow;
Until the appointed time the Father says; Galatians 4:2.
Just as we are children in bondage of sin and shame;
The Devil has his way with us in the world; Galatians 4:3.
But when the fullness of God came forth he sent his Son;
Made of woman, made under the law; Galatians 4:4.
To redeem those that were under the law of Moses;
That we might receive the adoption of sons; Galatians 4:5.
Because we are now sons, God sent forth his Spirit;
So in our hearts we can cry, Abba, Father; Galatians 4:6.
Therefore we are not like the servant, but we are a son;
And being a son, then an heir of God through Jesus; Galatians 4:7.
Would you rather be a son to God, or a servant to Satan?
The choice is yours while living on this earthly world.
When you die, the choice you made is the one to be judged.
Accept Jesus and be a son, or: stay worldly and be in torment.
Through Jesus' death in bringing many sons unto glory;
To make the captain of their salvation in suffering; Hebrews 2:10.
For those who followed Satan and the Antichrist and received the mark;
The smoke of their torment will ascend forever; Revelation 14:9-11.

William T. Smith

God's Gift

We have a gift from God Almighty; If we choose to accept it.
This gift is very precious, you accept it or you don't and lose it.
The gift is the gift of life, not just physical, but eternal life.
You accept this gift by accepting God's Son, (Jesus Christ).
To do this you must ask God to forgive the sin in your life.
With an honest and willing heart, this will make Jesus your Savior.
Because: We can never rewrite what we have done in our life.
But: Through Jesus we can write a new beginning starting this hour.

William T. Smith

Christmas is Wonderful

Christmas is the most wonderful time of the year.
It is when the churches declares the birth of Jesus.
They do this with an Nativity scene with glad cheer.
And all of earth does know that we are most blessed.
We go to church and hear all the wonderful things;
that is associated with Jesus and His gift to mankind.
We go around town and sing all these Christmas carols.
In hope that it makes someone happy and with giving.
Then we go uptown and see Santa Clause in his house.
Where the children are telling him all their wishes.
And everybody forgets what Christmas is all about.
As they are drinking and giving Santa a big shout.

William T. Smith

God Gives a Gift

God wants to give us a gift that everyone really wants.

But: it seems no one is willing to accept this one gift.

The gift is eternal life in glory with Him (Jesus Christ).

Maybe it is not the gift they refuse, but: the gift giver.

God sent His Son Jesus to earth as the gift giver to man.

And we do hear of people trying to live a longer life.

Why not just accept the gift of eternal life from God?

Do you think that serving Jesus here on earth is to much?

Think about it: Serve Jesus as your Savior here on earth.

And: in return be with Jesus forever in a place of glory.

In glory you will be like God; in most every way possible.

And: is not that what we really want in this life for today?

We do every thing possible to be a god here on earth any way.

Why not give yourself over to the real God, and be like Him?

William T. Smith

Forgiven Forever

F - is for forever: You belong to God for an limitless time.

O- is for original: You are a copy of what Jesus has done.

R- is for repentance: You dedicate your life for and to Jesus.

G- is for God: Who is perfect in power, wisdom and goodness.

I- is for invite: God offers His salvation to all who will ask.

V- is for vindicate: Jesus sets you free; delivered you from sin.

E- is for earthly: Jesus takes you from earthly favor, to Godly.

N- is for Nativity: A place you were thought of in Gods glory.

F- is for forgiven: God gives you an unconditional pardon.

O- is for only: God's final outcome to pay for your sin.

R- is for redeemed: God through Jesus bought you back.

E- is for everlasting: God's grace for you is eternal; forever.

V- is for victory: God assumed your punishment for your sin.

E- is for eternal: You will have an infinite duration with God.

R- is for restitution: God restored man to his previous state.

We are forgiven forever when we accept Jesus as our savior.
We are restored from the sin of Adam, to the grace of God.

William T. Smith

Faith or Wisdom

Your faith should never stand in the wisdom of man.
But: your faith should be in the power of God Almighty.
When you speak the wisdom of God; it is a mystery.
This is what God ordained before the world; to our glory.
I speak and teach without enticing words of man's wisdom.
But: when I speak, I pray it is a demonstration of the Spirit.
I came to Jesus, not to receive the evil spirit of this world.
I come to Jesus for the wisdom of God; given in His word.
God has chosen the foolish things of this world we live in.
To confuse the wise of this world, so the wise will look foolish.
For it is written: Eye has not seen, nor the ear has not heard;
the things that God has prepared for those who love Him.

William T. Smith

The Reason

The church says that Jesus is the reason
That we celebrate the Christmas season.
Jesus is the reason we give gifts that day.
For God gave us a gift called eternal life.
If we want this gift of eternal life, we must accept it.
We accept it by asking Jesus to forgive us of the sin.
After we do that, we can now use God's gift of peace.
Read the Bible, pray, study and live life right.
When death comes to this earthly body, and it will.
We have an eternal body that will live in eternity.
Now for those who do not accept this marvelous gift.
You will still have an eternal body; but it will be death.
You will not be in glory celebrating with Jesus Christ.
You will be in torment, screaming "Why did I not believe".
The choice is yours to make while alive on this planet.
Make the right choice now, while you still have life.

William T. Smith

Right Time

This is the right time, even though it may be a sad time.
You lost a loved one, But: Jesus is the way to let Him shine.
This is the right time, and it is a very joyous and happy time.
There is a marriage to attend and Jesus is there in the subline.
This is the right time, no matter what you are going threw.
For Jesus came to heal the sick, and to give happiness to you.
Blessed are the poor in spirit: for theirs is the kingdom of heaven.
Blessed are they that mourn: for they shall be comforted.
Blessed are the merciful: for they shall obtain mercy. Jesus said this.
The sermon on the mount, found in Matthew chapter 5.

William T. Smith

Jehovah

Jehovah is God Almighty; The Great I AM that I AM.

The God of Abraham, Isaac and Jacob, the one and same.

The letters of I AM is capitalized for He is the LORD.

The letters of LORD is capitalized for He is Jehovah.

Jehovah is LORD of all; who is Jesus the Son of God.

Jesus means: "God is with us", God in the fleshly form.

LORD told Abraham that of him would be a great nation.

He also said: "I will bless those who will bless Abraham".

Also He would curse those, who will curse Abraham.

But: Most of all Jehovah would bless all families of earth.

He did this when Jesus came to the earth as the Messiah.

As Messiah; Jesus had to die for the sin of this world.

When Jesus done this; He was crowned the King of the Jews.

So prophecy in Revelation 6:2 came to pass that day.

Now all people, in every country around this whole earth;

can be blessed, when they accept Jesus as their Lord and King.

Blessing and honor; Power to the one that sits on the throne.

This also fulfills the quote in Revelation 5:13, and other places.

Trust in the LORD JEHOVAH forever and forever and always.

For only in the LORD JEHOVAH is everlasting strength.

As it is written in Isiah 26:4; Trust in the LORD always.

Jesus is the way, the truth, the door unto salvation and His glory.

William T. Smith

Jehovah-M'Kaddesh

Jehovah-M'Kaddesh means: "The God who sanctifies".

Sanctify means: to set aside or to free from sin; purify.

We should keep the sabbath day to sanctify it. Deuteronomy 5:12.

So how do we sanctify the sabbath day? By keeping it Holy.

Before I formed you in the belly, I sanctified you. Jeremiah 1:5.

Another word for sanctified is consecrate or to make sacred.

In order to make sacred or to purify; you must grow in grace.

Therefore if a man purge himself from evil; He is a usable vessel.

One that has honor and sanctified for every good work. II Timothy 2:21.

Sanctify them through My truth: My word is truth. John 17:17.

Sanctify the LORD God in your heart,

and be ready to answer when asked;

Do it with reverence unto the question with meekness. I Peter 3:15.

Jesus gave himself for us, that he might redeem us from iniquity;

And purify us unto himself a peculiar people in good works. Titus 2:14.

Wherefore Jesus suffered without the gate,

to sanctify the people. Hebrews 13:12.

By which we are sanctified through

the blood of Jesus Christ. Hebrews 10:10.

Mercy unto you, and peace, and love be multiplied. Jude verse 2.

Jesus knows you and what you have done; Jesus still wants you.

William T. Smith

BOOK SIX

Being a Disciple

The dictionary states that a disciple is a follower.
A follower is a person in the service of another person.
A follower is also a person who imitates another.
To be Jesus' disciple you must imitate or follow Jesus.
If you follow Jesus, then you must also imitate Jesus.
In order to follow or imitate; you must have a relationship.
To have a relationship with Jesus, you must accept Him as Lord.
To accept Jesus as Lord, you must ask for His forgiveness.
To forgive all the sin and wrong doing that you ever done.
Then read the Bible and get to know Him personally as God.
Jesus said to go, preach, saying the kingdom of God is at hand.
Heal the sick, cleanse the lepers, raise the dead and;
cast out devils: You freely received, so freely give. Matthew 10.
Jesus also said that whosoever confess Him before men;
he will confess us before His Father which is in heaven.
So the person that takes up his cross and follows Jesus;
that person is a disciple of Christ Jesus: Matthew chapter 10.
If you do not take up your cross, you cannot be his disciple.

William T. Smith

Who is a Disciple?

The dictionary states that a disciple is in the inter circle.

To be in the inter circle of Christ; you must be His follower.

In order to be Jesus' follower; you must believe He is God.

In order to be in His inter circle; you must know Him personally.

Read your Bible, and get to know Jesus as your Lord and Savior.

Study the Bible, to show that you are approved to be His disciple.

For a disciple is not above his master; but follows his master.

When you have Jesus in your heart and soul you shall be perfect.

You are known by the spirit you have, and the message you give.

Jesus said that whosoever comes to him, he will not cast out.

But seek you first the kingdom of God, and your fruit will come.

For a tree grown by the water will bare good fruit.

Out of the abundance of your heart, your mouth will speak.

If your heart is of Jesus, then your treasure will be of Him.

A disciple must forgive those who have done him wrong.

But a disciple must not lie down and be silent. Luke chapter 6.

William T. Smith

What is a Disciple?

The dictionary states that a disciple is one that accepts;
and assists in the spreading the doctrine of another.
Paul preached Christ in the synagogues, in his day.
He preached that Christ was the Son of God, the Messiah.
The people that started to follow Christ, they got a nickname.
The disciples of Christ were called Christians first in Antioch.
God gave the gift of the Holy Spirit to all that believed.
So whosoever receives Jesus also receives the Holy Spirit.
A disciple of Jesus is to be a prophet or teacher of the word.
Separate your self from evil works and be joined with Christ.
A disciple is an offspring of God, but should not think highly.
When a disciple thinks more highly of himself, he leaves God out.
When you leave God out, then you will become like the world.
Nor think that the Godhead is like unto gold, silver or stone.
A disciple is a person instructed in the way of the Lord.
He should also be fervent in the Spirit and teach diligently.
A disciple is one that will testify the gospel of grace of God.
And must not shun to declare unto the people the counsel of God.
Speak with confidence, the Lord Christ Jesus about His word.
And do your best to make disciples of all believers of God.
Some will believe you, others will not and go their own way.
All of this is about accepting and assisting in the word of God.

William T. Smith

Education's Purpose

There is a saying by Malcolm Forbes that goes like this.
Education's purpose is to replace an empty mind with an open one.
Malcolm with this saying has a lot of truth in it for Christians.
We as humans have an empty mind when it comes to God and Jesus.
No matter if we read the Bible and try to understand the words there in.
We lack to understand; because we do not have an opened mind.
When it comes to spiritual things, we lack the knowledge of scripture.
When we ask Jesus in faith believing, then our mind begins to open.
The wisdom of God will start to fill the empty mind that we have.
Just as a teacher in school tries to open the mind of the student.
The Spirit of God will start opening the mind of a child of God.
Knowledge comes to a person when they start to understand the writing.
Understanding comes when the person get wisdom that God gives.
And wisdom comes when the person ask Jesus to forgive their sin.
Because understanding and knowledge is a gift that comes with wisdom.
The gift of wisdom comes when you accept Jesus as Lord and Savior.
With this gift of wisdom is also the gift of eternal life with Jesus.
Eternal life comes when you accept the salvation of Jesus' forgiveness.

William T. Smith

Who Would I Blame?

As I was washing the dishes; I had a tea stained pitcher.

I decided to put bleach into it; that will lift the stain.

About that time the telephone started ringing, my hand full.

The grandchildren started to fight and scream over something.

As this was going on, I was swishing the bleach in the pitcher.

My finger slipped, and the bleach landed on my good T-shirt.

The bleach left a big stain on the front of my new blue T-shirt.

Who should I blame for all this commotion, or was it an accident.

Really: nobody was to blame, but: I needed to blame someone.

So: I would blame myself, for I made the choice to use bleach.

I chose to use bleach on a tea stained plastic pitcher in the first place.

I was the one who chose to swish it around to get rid of the stain.

The grandchildren and the telephone may have contributed a little.

But it was me who was washing the dishes, and with bleach no less.

William T. Smith

What is so Special About the Bible?

One: It is the word of God; spiritually inspired by God.

Two: It is the history of God's chosen nation of Israel.

Three: It is the redeeming power over the sin in our life.

Four: It is the prophecy of what will happen in the future.

Five: It tells how the earth, man and universe was created.

Six: It tells how man fell from grace, and became a sinner.

Seven: It tells about repentance and the after life of man.

Eight: It tells us about an evil spirit, Lucifer, called Satan.

Nine: It shows how mankind should live while on earth.

Ten: It shows how to have and live by faith in your life.

Eleven: It shows how to receive eternal life with Jesus.

Twelve: It lets us know about forgiveness of sin, if we ask.

Thirteen: It tells us know about a place called glory or heaven.

Fourteen: It lets us know about a place of torment called hell.

This is a short list of how special the Book called Holy Bible Is.

I would not trade this book for anything, for it gives me peace.

William T. Smith

One Thing I Desire

One thing I do really desire of my LORD, Jesus.
And I will seek after all of my days here on earth.
That I may dwell in the house of my LORD, Jesus.
All my days, and behold the beauty of my LORD.
To inquire His presence, and His wisdom always.
For the LORD is my light and my salvation of soul.
The LORD is my strength in all I do in this life.
Of whom shall I be afraid, of whom shall I fear.
Teach me your ways LORD, and lead me not astray.
Then I will cry out unto you, LORD you are my rock.
Let me not be silent of you all my days here on earth.
Let you not be silent in me, while I am here on earth.
Blessed be my LORD, because He does hear my prayer.
My LORD sits on the Mercy Seat as my advocate.

William T. Smith

Our Children

Jesus said "Suffer the little children to come unto me;
Forbid them not: for such is the kingdom of God".
Listen to the child, they will say what is in there heart.
Come as a little child, and I will in no wise cast you out.
The children's children is the crown of the grandparents.
But the glory of the children, comes from their father.
All children are an heritage unto the Lord God Almighty.
The fruit of the womb is the reward of both God and man.
For in the beginning God created male and female alike.
He told them to go and multiply and replenish the earth.
When ever you conceive a child, it is a gift from God.
Teach your child to respect man and God his creator of life.
When you grow old, they will kept the sparkle in your eye.
You wont be grieved with the evil that come without discipline.

William T. Smith

Trouble

Pray to God now, while God can be found in your life.

For when trouble comes, you will be prepared to endure.

Acknowledge the sin you have to the Lord, hide it not.

Confess your iniquity and transgressions unto the Lord.

The Lord will forgive you of all the things you have done.

When trouble comes, you will hide in the arms of the Lord.

Compress about Jesus with songs of your deliverance of sin.

Give praise unto the Lord with love songs and fervent prayer.

Do not wait until trouble strikes you hard, and you go down.

Give yourself over to the Son (Jesus) the Messiah, the Christ.

Then get ready to fight, for Satan will bring you much trouble.

Fight with the Holy Spirit, the words of God, it is in the Bible.

William T. Smith

Covered Sin

The Holy Heavenly Father cannot see your sin.

When you have the Lord Jesus Christ living within.

Our Heavenly Father cannot look on sin, he is Holy.

Through Jesus he can look at us, Jesus paid the price.

We must have a new spiritual body at our human death.

Because we would not be able to look at a Holy Father.

Out of the ground you were taken, return to dust at death.

Dust you are, and dust you shall return; Genesis 3:19.

You were born in a natural body, while here on earth.

You will be raised into a spiritual body, at you death.

There is a natural or physical body, as you live on earth.

There is a spiritual body in eternity. I Corinthians 15: 44.

Blessed is he whose transgression is forgiven. Psalms 32:1.

By the blood shed by Jesus your sin is covered, if you ask.

As I live says the LORD; every knee, and every tongue will;

Bow down before me and confess "I Am God"; Romans 14:11.

Everyone will give account of what they done unto a Holy God.

You cannot do this in a natural body, it has to be spiritual body.

Jesus covers your spiritual body with his blood if you accept him.

If you do not accept Jesus as Lord and Savior, you will be naked.

Standing naked before a Holy God, who can see all your iniquity.

William T. Smith

Holy Spirit

For there are three that bear record in heaven.
The three are: the Father, the Word, and the Holy Spirit.
As there are three that bear witness in earth.
These are; the spirit, the water, and the blood.
But the Comforter, which is the Holy Spirit, whom
the Father will send in Jesus' name, he will teach
you all things, and bring things to your remembrance.
The Holy Spirit is a Comforter, sent from heaven to teach.
Paul was forbidden of the Holy Spirit to preach in Asia.
The Holy Spirit is also an Instructor or a guide in your life.
The Spirit itself bears witness with our spirit, her on earth.
That we shall know that we are the children of God.
I tell you the truth, my conscience bears witness
with the Holy Spirit, so that I cannot lie to you.
The Holy Spirit is a Quickener and a Sanctifier.
The Holy Spirit sent by God in the intercessor
that quickens your spirit to come to the Son (Jesus).
This is found in; I John, John, Acts, Romans, and Isaiah.

William T. Smith

Trinity – Third Person

The definition of the Holy Spirit in Websters Dictionary.

Holy Spirit: The third person of the Trinity. Holy Spirit.

Comforter: One that gives comfort. Holy Spirit, Solace.

Instructor: One that instructs, to teach or command.

Guide: One who directs a person in his conduct or course.

Sanctifier: Set apart to a sacred purpose. Purify, Holy Spirit.

Quickener: To make alive. To shine more brightly. Revive.

Intercessor: The act of interceding. Prayer, Petition.

Teacher: One who teaches or instructs. To make known.

Sent: To cause to issue. To cause to happen. Delight, Transmit.

This is what the dictionary says about the Holy Spirits gift.

If you know Jesus, you know the Father, and the Holy Spirit.

The three are one, and the one is three, Almighty God Creator.

William T. Smith

Plan of Salvation

Do you understand what it takes for a person to go to Heaven?
Consider how the Bible answers this question: It's a matter of FAITH.

F IS FOR FORGIVENESS
We cannot have eternal life and heaven
without God's forgiveness.   Read Ephesians 1:7a

A IS FOR AVAILABLE
Forgiveness is available. It is
*Available for all.   Read John 3:16
*But not automatic.   Read Matthew7:21a

I IS FOR IMPOSSIBLE
It is impossible for God to allow sin into heaven.
*Because of who He is: God is loving and just.
His judgment is against sin.   Read James 2:13a
*Because of who we are:
Every person is a sinner.   Read Romans 3:23

But how can a sinful person enter heaven, when God allows no sin?

T IS FOR TURN
Turn means to repent.
*Turn from something—sin and self.   Read Luke 13:3b
*Turn to Someone; trust Christ only.   Read Romans 10:9

H IS FOR HEAVEN
Heaven is eternal life.
*Here.   Read John 10:10b

*Hereafter.   Read John 14:3

How can a person have God's forgiveness, heaven and eternal life, and Jesus as personal Savior and Lord? By trusting in Christ and asking Him for forgiveness. Take the step of faith described by another meaning of FAITH: Forsaking All I Trust Him. You must believe with a willing honest heart unto the Lord.

Prayer:

Lord Jesus, I know I am a sinner and have displeased You in many ways. I believe You died for my sin and only through faith in Your death and resurrection can I be forgiven. I want to turn from my sin and ask You to come into my life as my Savior and Lord. From this day on, I will follow You by living a life that pleases You. Thank You, Lord Jesus for saving me. Amen.

After you have received Jesus Christ into life, tell a Christian friend about this important decision you have made. Follow Christ in believer's baptism and church membership. Grow in your faith and enjoy new friends in Christ by becoming part of His church. There, you'll find others who will love and support you.

Highway To Heaven

You won't find it on a map, but a highway to heaven does exist. "The Roman Road" is explained in the Bible, and it tells how to go to heaven.

We need God's power because we have a problem with sin. "For all have sinned and fall short of the glory of God" (Romans 3:23). "Sin" means missing the mark or missing God's intended destination for us. None of us can reach that destination on his or her own because everyone is a sinner.

When we work, we earn money. Sin earns wages as well—wages of death. Because God loves all sinners, He has provided another route: "For the wages of sin is death, but the gift of God is eternal life in Christ Jesus our Lord" (Romans 6:23).

The highway to heaven is found in Romans 10:9: "If you confess with your mouth, "Jesus is Lord", and believe in your heart that God raised Him from the dead, you will be saved." We need to confess our sin and ask God for forgiveness. To confess Jesus as Lord involves agreeing with God about your sin and your need for salvation. You must repent of your sin, turning away from the direction in life in which you are going. To "believe in your heart" is to place your faith in Jesus, trusting that He died on a cross to forgive your sins. "But God proves His own love for us in that while we were still sinners Christ died for us" (Romans 5:8).

If you would like to have salvation in Jesus Christ, sincerely pray a prayer like this one, being honest in your heart and believing that Jesus is God's only Son: " Dear God, I confess to You my sin and need for salvation. I turn away from my sin and place my faith in Jesus as my Savior and Lord. Amen".

Share your faith in Jesus with a Christian friend or pastor. Becoming a Christian is your first step on the lifelong road of spiritual growth and service God desires for you. Follow Christ in believer's baptism by immersion and join a local church.

A Gospel Worker
My version of John 3:14-21

And as Moses lifted up the serpent in the wilderness, even so must Jesus the Son of man be lifted up: That whosoever believes in Jesus should not perish, but have eternal life.

 For God so loved mankind, the he gave is only begotten Son, that whosoever believes in Jesus should not perish, but have everlasting life. For God sent not his Son (Jesus) into the world to condemn mankind: but that mankind through him might be saved.

He that believes on Jesus is not condemned: but he that believes not is condemned already, because he did not believe in the name of the only begotten Son of God. And this is the condemnation,

that light is come into the world, and mankind loved darkness rather than light, because their deeds were evil. For everyone that does evil hates the light, neither comes to the light, lest his deeds should be reproved, or corrected.

But he that does truth comes to the light, that his deeds may be made manifest, that they are wrought or fashioned in God.

In him (Jesus) was life; and the life was the light of men. John 1:4.

After reading this you may want to go back and read the Highway to Heaven again, with Jesus; the light;being on your mind.

BOOK SEVEN

Hear Me When I Call

Hear me when I call, O God of my righteousness.
You have enlarged me when I was in distress.
Please have mercy on me, and hear my prayer.
Lead me, O Lord, in my righteousness of your Son.
Make your way straight before my face, Holy Father.
Have mercy on me, O Lord; for I am tired and weak.
O Lord, please heal me; for my bones are troubled.
I will praise you, O Lord, with my whole heart.
I will tell everyone of all your marvelous works.
Preserve me, Holy Father, for in you I put my trust.
For you Lord Jesus, you are my rock, and my fortress.
You are my deliver, my God, my strength, who I trust.
You are my shield, and the sword of my salvation.
Look at the heavens, and how they declare your glory.
Look around at nature, how they show your handy work.
Let your name be exalted in the glory and power of God.
And I will sing of your praise in the salvation you show.

William T. Smith

My God, My God

My God, my God why have you forsaken me?
Why are you so far from helping me with this?
Why are you not hearing the loudness of my words?
All that see me are laughing me to scorn, by this.
They sneer at me while shaking their evil heads.
Please do not be this far away from me in my trouble.
This trouble has came, and there is no one to help.
Lord, hear me O Lord, when I cry out with my voice.
Have mercy on me Lord, answer me with this plea.
Teach me your ways Lord, and lead me in your path.
Unto you I pray, you are my rock, I cannot be silent.
When I am silent my endeavors brings me way down.
In you Lord, do I put my hope and desire and trust.
Let me never be ashamed of your glory and righteousness.
Blessed is he whose transgression and sin is forgiven.
I acknowledge my sin unto you and hid not my iniquity.
I confess my transgressions unto to Lord of my salvation.
Many are my afflictions from the wicked one, called Satan.
But: you Lord Jesus, have delivered me from all of them.

William T. Smith

Little Children Come Close

Little children come close, I want you to hear.
A story about me, that I hold very very dear.
I was talking one night to the evil one, our enemy.
When the Lord called and said: This is for all eternity.
For you see, I was full of hate, pride and was very hurt.
The enemy I let in, and in my thoughts he did lurk.
He wanted me to murder, and was laughing with glee.
Then Jesus asked if this is the I wanted to feel in eternity.
I knew who was talking to me at that time of night.
I did not have to think about it at all; No, I want the light.
I started to pray for Jesus to forgive me of all my sin.
Come into my heart and soul, I want you to live with-in.
But: I had to ask for help for the ones I needed to forgive.
I realized they also needed forgiveness in order to live.
Jesus came into my heart that night, out in the street.
Now I have peace, and joy and love that cannot be beat.

William T. Smith

Vows

A vow is something you promises to do, or declare.
When you make a vow; you are bound by that vow.
If you make a vow you know you will not keep it.
Then that vow is worse than just telling a big lie.
So it would be better, that you did not make the vow.
Then to vow and not keep it. Ecclesiastes 5:4-5.
When you say the pledge of allegiance to the flag.
You are making a vow unto the country of that flag.
When you make a vow unto the Lord, you are declaring;
or making a pledge to do whatever is in your heart.
Keep that vow, pledge, declaration to the best you can.
Never say it was a mistake or you did not mean to do it.
The Lord looks at a pledge or vow with honor and joy.
Breaking that vow, dishonors the Lord and yourself.

William T. Smith

A Talking Donkey

You may have heard of: Francis the talking mule.

Or maybe of Mister Ed, the talking horse.

The most popular is the serpent of Adam and Eve.

But have you ever heard of a talking donkey?

While Moses was leading the children of Israel in the wilderness.

They came upon the land of Moab, this side of the Jordan by Jericho.

The Moabites were afraid because there was so many Israelites.

And Balak the son of Zippor was the King of Moab.

He talked to Balaam the son of Beor, to curse the Israelite people.

God told Balaam not to curse the people, or to go with the King.

But Balaam saddled his donkey to go with the King of Moab.

The donkey saw the angel of the Lord, standing in the way.

The donkey turned aside and went into a field off the beaten path.

Balaam smote the donkey, and went the way of the vineyards.

But the angel of the Lord was there also to stop them from going on.

The donkey seen the angel, and thrust herself into the wall.

When this happened Balaam's foot crushed against the wall.

So Balaam smote the donkey the second time, because of his foot.

At this the angel of the Lord stopped the donkey in a narrow path.

The donkey seen the angel and fell down under Ballam.

Balaam's anger was kindled and he smote the donkey with his staff.

The Lord opened the mouth of the donkey and said to Balaam:

What have I done to you, that you smote me three times?

And Balaam said: Because you have mocked me three times;

If I had a sword I would kill you right here, in the path.

The donkey said: Am I not your donkey that you ride on.

The Lord opened the eyes of Balaam to see the angel of the Lord.

Balaam bowed down his head, and laid his face flat on the ground.

The angel said: go with them, but say only what I tell you.

When Balak saw them, he offered Balaam ox and sheep for the curse.

But Balaam said: I cannot curse the children of Israel over this.

For the Lord has for bidden me to do so. Numbers chapter 22- 23- 24.

William T. Smith

Guardian Angel

If we believe it or not; we do have an angel over us.

The angel of his presents saved them: in his love;

And in his pity he redeemed them; and he bare them,

And carried them all the days of old; Isaiah 63:9.

The angel of the Lord camps around you; Psalms 34:7.

Come little children, I will teach you reverence unto the Lord.

Reverence the Lord, and the Lord will deliver. Psalms 34:11.

For he shall give his angels charge over you; Psalms 91:11.

Do not despise any child, for their angels behold their face;

And the face of the Father which is in heaven; Matthew 18:10.

And I beheld and heard the voice of many angels. Revelation 5:11.

Do not forget to entertain strangers, for some are angels. Hebrews 13: 2.

Yes: We have an angel watching over us, and protecting us.

But beware; not all angels are good, some are evil; Jude verse 6.

William T. Smith

Mentor

The dictionary says; that a mentor is a trusted adviser.
A mentor will provide guidance, motivation, and role modeling;
Emotional support, to help someone explore, or identify.
The Bible talks about mentors from Genesis to Revelation.
When you help someone to understand the Bible more clearly;
That is being a mentor, for you are showing that person, Jesus.
When a person gets a clearer understanding of who Jesus is;
To the point they want the tell others, you have done God's will.

William T. Smith

What Will I Do In Heaven?

I shall run and not be weary; I shall walk and not faint.

The body that I shall receive, will be complete in heaven.

The Lord has set a table before me, in the house where I dwell.

There will be plenty for me to eat for the table will never be bare.

I can drink from the pure river of water, in the mist of the street.

The twelve fruits from the trees planted by the river I can eat.

I will be comforted and be comfortable in the presents of the Lord.

For Jesus will take away the desire of my eyes in a heartbeat.

So that I will neither mourn nor weep or have tears on my cheek.

But I will be attending a wedding; the marriage of the Lamb.

So what will I do in Heaven? Praising and Glorifying my Lord.

Praising him for dying for me; Glorifying him for saving me.

All of this means only one thing, in heaven Jesus is throwing a party.

The angels will be there as servants of the Lord, at his wedding.

I will be one of the guest at this party, for I accepted the invitation.

I will have a body that will not get weary or will it ever get tired.

There is a table set with plenty of food, and a river to drink from.

There will be no tears for those who did not make it to the wedding.

When you go to a wedding, are you thinking of those who are not there?

And this party will last through out all of eternity in heaven with Jesus.

William T. Smith

What is Eternal Death?

Eternal death is being without the presents of God.
Eternal death is being without any love whatsoever.
Eternal death is not having hope, in the place your in.
Eternal death is not having friends or family to be with.
In the Bible, death and hell were cast into a lake of fire.
Just think about that for a while, is that what you want.
Being in a lake of fire, without love, hope, or the Lord.
That makes me wonder, Why people choose not to believe?
Heaven is just the opposite of torment with no escape.
In heaven you will have love, hope, peace, joy with God.
All you have to do is believe Jesus is the Son of God in flesh.
Ask Jesus to forgive you for disobeying his commandments.
Jesus' commandments are not grievous, nor hard to follow.
Love the Lord your God with all your heart and soul.
And love your neighbor as you love yourself, always.
Anybody can do those two commandments, give it a try.

William T. Smith

Redbird

Redbird- redbird are you making your nest in my tree.

You will have plenty of company; other nest you can see.

The ground is fertile- and the grass is very green and cut.

There are plenty of worms, and bugs for you to eat.

Finding twigs and old grass to build your nest is all around.

Now comes the feeding and the chirping and the fun.

For in these trees, is where all of God's birds belong.

Rejoicing in the springtime, while singing your praise songs.

This is one way God rewards me, while sitting here at home.

That way the Virus-19 hopefully will leave me alone.

This Virus-19 will be gone someday and so will all of you.

In the meantime, we both have a lot of work and living to do.

God created you for this purpose, in this world we live in.

He created me to help care for you, while I serve Him on earth.

William T. Smith

Life Tips

"What ever you do: Do not pray for an easy life.
Pray for the strength to endure a difficult one". Bruce Lee.
When you have an easy life, look where you compromised.
For an easy life may mean you are not in the will of the Lord.
"The grass will wither, and the flowers will fade.
But: the word of God shall stand forever". Isaiah 40:8.
We are like the flowers and the grass, we will die.
If we have the word of God In us, we will live eternally
"Submit yourself therefore to God, (In all things).
Resist the Devil, and he will flee from you". James 4:7.
If you are totally committed to God, you already have victory.
Tell Satan to flee in the name of Jesus, Satan cannot stay.
Cast all your cares upon Him, (Jesus our Savior and Lord).
For Jesus cares for you, (That He died for you). I Peter 5:7
When the burdens and cares of this life is getting you down.
Remember that Jesus loves you more than you may realize.

William T. Smith

Savior or Slave

What is Jesus to you? Is he a Savior or a Slave?
I have heard sermons and listened to prayers in church.
I have noticed that Jesus; to a lot of people is a slave.
It seems that they are always wanting something done.
But never hear of a praise of what Jesus has or is doing.
The Bible states that these prayers are made a mist.
Meaning that it is what I want; and not what God desires.
Jesus came to earth to be our Savior, our King and Lord.
He took on himself our sin, and our shame, to give life.
We need nothing else from Jesus our Lord, just serve Him.
Accept the promises He has given for just believing in Him.
Eternal life in glory or heaven, is more reward, that He shows.
So: is Jesus going to be your Savior, of all your sin and shame.
Or: is Jesus going to be your slave of all your wants and desires.

William T. Smith

BOOK EIGHT

The God I Serve

The God I serve walks and talks with me always.
Not like he did with Adam and Eve in the garden.
They heard the voice of God walking in the garden.
God always came to them, in the cool of the evening.
This is found in Genesis chapters two and three.
And Enoch walked with God three hundred years;
After he fathered Methuselah, his eldest son.
For Enoch walked with God: and he was not:
This is found in Genesis 5:22-24, of the genealogy.
Noah was a just man and perfect in his generations.
And Noah walked with God. Genesis 6:9.
Sometimes God sends his angels to speak for him.
And the angel of the Lord said unto her, this was Hagar.
I will multiply your seed exceedingly, or abundantly.
That it shall not be numbered for multitude. Genesis 16:10.
Jacob wrestled with a man of God, who changed his name.
Jacob's name was changed to Israel. Genesis 32:28.
This is the same God that I serve today; Lord Jesus Christ.
He talks to me from nature, children, Bible in many ways.
Everything does not always go the way I would like.
But that is because God does not want to see me harmed.

William T. Smith

Beautiful Son

Beautiful Son; Jesus the one I love and adore.
Beautiful Son; Jesus you are my strength my core.
Beautiful Son; Christ Jesus did died on a cruel cross.
Beautiful Son; Jesus came to earth to save the lost.
Beautiful Son; Jesus did not stay in that grave.
Beautiful Son; the one that rose on the third day.
Beautiful Son; sitting on the right hand of the Father.
Beautiful Son; my advocate, lawyer, and go between.
Beautiful Son; the one that gives me a glories peace.
Beautiful Son; thank you for the comforter, Holy Spirit.
Beautiful Son; Jesus is making me a home in heaven.
Beautiful Son; Jesus will build you one, if you accept Him.

William T. Smith

A Pleasant Day

I had a very good and pleasant day today.
My telephone at home is where it stayed.
Where I was, things was peaceful and quiet.
I was very happy and this I did like.
When I left and headed for my home.
I found where I left that annoying phone.
I checked to see if anyone had called.
This I found was thirty-five missed calls.
I checked to see how many messages I had.
But: not a single message was left, how sad.
They were all what we call a robo call.
The number is out of service on them all.
But oh what a very pleasant day I really had.
Jesus talked to me, that is why I was so glad.
I will enjoy the bliss up there in God's heaven.
For I know, no telephone will enter there-in.

William T. Smith

Afraid

Only when we are afraid, do we begin to live.

A saying of a lady named: Dorothy Thompson.

If a man die, shall he live again? Job 14:14.

When we are no longer afraid of death, is:

When we have accepted Jesus as our Savior.

I shall not die, but live and declare the works of the Lord.

David wrote this in a psalm, read Psalm 118:17.

I am alive with Jesus in my heart; I will declare his love.

Lord by these things men live, and is the life of my spirit.

You will recover me, and make me to live. Isaiah 38:16.

Incline your ear, and come unto me: and your soul shall live.

And I will make an everlasting covenant with you. Isaiah 55:3.

By what Jesus done on the cross at Calvary, we shall live.

By His blood, God makes an everlasting covenant with us.

That covenant is that He will never leave or forsake us.

The covenant is broken if we willing forsake Christ Jesus.

For to me life is Christ, and to die is gain. Philippians 1:23.

I accepted Christ as my Savior; I live for Him, I die to the world.

William T. Smith

Creative Block

Every now and then, I come up with this creative block.
It may be caused by many different things going on.
I have read what others do when this happens to them.
Some of them I do myself; others is a big distraction.
So: what I do is go to the book called the Holy Bible.
This book has so many stories, quotes, and suggestions.
After reading what God has to say about different things.
Then ask Jesus to help, with the inspiration of the Holy Spirit.
The Holy Spirit will give me the inspiration to keep going.
No matter if it is writing, painting or any other thing you do.
Creative Block is there, only because you let it stay there.
Do something you like, and the inspiration will come back.

William T. Smith

How Do We Worship?

Don't let worship be all about you – let it be about Jesus.
Always go to worship with wanting to get something from it.
If you don't receive anything, you may not be praising God.
The Bible tells us to not forsake going to church to worship.
But always go expecting to get something from the worship.
You do this when you talk to others about the message preached.
When you worship, worship with your spirit praising God.
This is the way only you can do it, for God knows your heart.
You may be excited and can't show it, some people are that way.
Another way to worship is in the offering that you bring to God.
Do not give so that you can be praised, give to praise the Lord.
Church is fellowship with one another not the church building.
Everybody worships in a different way, we are not all alike.
We are individuals made in the image of God, but different.
Some may sit calmly, others may dance, others clap their hands.
The way we worship is not as important as praising the Lord.
Never forsake worship, for in doing so you give Satan a foothold.
The pastor, the song leader, the usher are some that leads us.
We are not the audience, we are the children of Lord God.
When we go to worship, we fellowship with each other;
We sing songs, we pray for others, we give an offering.
We praise the Lord for what he has done, and going to do.
We listen to the message, all of this is part of worshiping God.
Forget about yourself, enjoy the service, worship Christ Jesus.

William T. Smith

Living a Holy Life

Living a holy life does not mean you cannot do any wrong.
What that is; is living a life the best you can for Lord Jesus.
Jesus lived to glorify the Father, you want to be like Jesus.
Jesus prayed or talked to the Father everyday of his life here.
The Word says: pray without ceasing, so think about Jesus.
What do you think, about the glory of God for helping you.
No matter what you do; always have Jesus' thoughts in mind.
Jesus should always be your first thought in times of trouble.
Jesus should always be your first thought in times of happiness.
Jesus should always be your first thought in going to work.
When you are at work, always keep Jesus in your thoughts.
On your way home from work, keep Jesus in your thoughts.
This is the way to live a holy life unto our Lord, Christ Jesus.
When you do, you will live forever with our Lord, Jesus.

William T. Smith

Being Saved

When you ask Jesus to forgive you of your sin.
When you say it with an honest heart: you are saved.
Saved means that your soul will be in glory with Jesus.
That is as soon as you accept Jesus, you will have peace.
This does not mean that you will not have temptations.
This means when temptations come; Jesus is there to help.
When Satan knows that you are a child of the living God.
He will throw things at you that will make you doubt God.
When this happens and it will, remember your place with God.
The peace you have with Lord Jesus will over-come Satan.
Tell Satan to depart from you, for you want to live like Jesus.
How did Jesus live? He lived to glorify His Father in heaven.
Our Holy Father sees what you are going through every day.
That is why he sent the Holy Spirit to be with you at all times.
The Lord Jesus is your advocate unto our Holy Father God.
The Holy Spirit is your comforter in the time of trouble.

William T. Smith

Peace with God

Therefore being justified by faith, we have peace with God.

Because we rejoice in the grace and hope of Lord Jesus Christ.

All these things Jesus has spoken, so you might have peace.

The world will give you tribulation, Jesus has overcome the world.

Jesus gives you peace, not like the world gives; peace with trouble.

So do not let your heart be troubled, neither let it be afraid.

Let the peace of God rule in your heart, your soul, your mind.

To which also you are called in one body, be you thankful.

For Jesus is our peace, and made us one with him, no walls.

So our feet should be shod with the preparation of peace in Jesus.

So we can go and preach peace to others, being here or far away.

Because whosoever calls upon the Lord Jesus shall be saved.

But: How can they call on Jesus, whom they have never believed?

And; How shall they believe in Jesus, when they have never heard?

So: How can they hear with out a preacher telling them about Jesus?

But: How can one preach, unless that one is sent to preach Jesus?

Oh how beautiful are the feet of them that preach the gospel?

The one that brings glad tidings of good things from Lord Jesus.

May the grace of God be multiplied unto you this day of peace.

Through the knowledge of God and Jesus Christ our Lord and Savior.

William T. Smith

Son of God

I have a beautiful Son shining in my soul today.

Jesus the Son of God gives me peaceful joy untold.

Jesus forgave me of my sin and shame when I asked.

He took it off my shoulders and never gave it back.

Jesus can do the same thing for you, if you believe.

Jesus is God in the flesh, and wants to save you and me.

Save us from what? Eternal death in a place called hell.

That is why Jesus came to the earth, for our redemption.

For God loves mankind so much in sent his Son Jesus;

To be punished for our sin and disobedience to Him.

Jesus is always with you, day and night, your not alone.

When we die, our soul and spirit will have a new body.

One where we can stand before Father God Almighty.

It is an eternal body of life in Jesus, or death in Satan.

I want Him to say: Well done my faithful servant.

I do not want to hear: Depart from me you doer of evil.

William T. Smith

A Relationship

My wife at my side, she will never stand anymore.
She divorced me and married now to another man.
I am a single man that is free to date and marry again.
If and when I do marry again, it will not be a sinful act.
For I will still have only one woman, not my divorced.
That does not mean that I am looking for a new mate.
But that does mean I am waiting on the Lord for a mate.
The Lord himself said: It is not good for man to be alone.
We are made for a relationship with one another, together.
When we are in the right relationship here on earth.
Then we can be in the right relationship with Christ Jesus.
A married couple (man with woman) has God's blessing.
When the couple has Jesus as their Savior, it is heaven.

William T. Smith

Wrestle a Pig

I learned long ago never wrestle with a pig.
You get dirty, and besides the pig likes it. Cyrus Ching.
That is what happens to a person that lives in sin.
You really get dirty, and besides Satan really likes it.
So stay out of the pig pen, unless you have to work there.
And if you work there, don't wrestle with those pigs.
A person in sin does not have to stay in that sinful place.
We have an advocate named Jesus to get you out of there.
Sometimes as a Christian, we have to work in dirty places.
But that does not mean, we have to do it like the others.
When we work in a sinful place, represent Jesus there.
Someone may come to know the Lord, if you act differently.
For Jesus went where the sinners were to receive one.
We are all sinners, a Christian is cleaned by Jesus' blood.
Jesus died on the cross to save the sinner from hell.
He did not come to punish the sinful, but to redeem them.

William T. Smith

BOOK NINE

Be a Soldier

When Jesus ask you to do something; He will equip you to do so.
Because Jesus usually ask what He knows is out of your comfort zone.
Saying that, Jesus also said: Love one another as I have loved you.
To help in our love we should not forsake to assemble together regular.
For in assembling together, we can exhort with one another in Christ.
So that what one says, may be what another needs to hear at that time.
When we do these two things- love one another- do God's bidding.
Then we show the world that we are indeed Jesus' disciples.
Do not love in word by your tongue, but in deeds and in truth.
Do not love just the Christian, but also the evil doer, this is sowing.
The more we sow, the more we can reap what we have been sowing.
We sow in love, we reap love, we sow in hate, we reap hate.
So let us sow in the Spirit of Jesus with the Holy Spirit leading us.
In this always remember; God is not mocked, so do not deceive.
Saying this, then we should make disciples of some around us.
That way we show our love, by letting them show their love.
But: in all things be fruitful and commit your witness to many.
By doing all you can; you become a soldier of Christ Jesus.

William T. Smith

Have Gratitude

We often take for granted the very things that most deserve our gratitude.

A very true saying in the world today, of an author named Cynthia Ozick.

This is true with both a Christian or a sinful person.

We take for granted the children and our life which God gave us.

We also take for granted our freedom in this country of America.

If you are a Christian, you most of the time probably take God for granted.

I do believe most people in this world think the world owes them.

But: we were put here to take care of this world we live in.

A married person usually takes their spouse for granted also.

Thinking the spouse is suppose to drop everything at their command.

But when you start being thankful, that is when you start to live.

Gratitude is a word for having thanksgiving for your very life.

Be grateful, respect others, work diligently, live peaceful with everyone.

This is what every person wants, but we do not work toward it.

Thank your spouse for what (he or she) is doing for you on a daily bases.

Thank God that he has given you life, and a world to live in.

Be grateful for who you have as well as what you have in your life.

In doing so: you will find that things are not as bad as you have thought.

William T. Smith

Joshua

Moses led the people of Israel for forty years.
Now it was time to process the promise land.
Moses died and a man named Joshua took over.
Joshua led the people through the Jordan River.
Just as Moses went across the Rea Sea on dry land.
Joshua went across the Jordan River on dry land.
Jericho was next on Joshua's list of people to conquer.
God told Joshua to march around the city for six days.
On the seventh day, march around seven times and shout.
When the children of Israel done this, the walls fell down.
From there Joshua defeated nation after nation for Israel.
Until the children of Israel took over all the promised land.
Then Joshua ran into a problem with the Israelites.
The Israelites wanted to serve the gods of these nations.
Joshua told the people: Choose this day who you will serve.
Will it be the gods of these nations that we have captured or:
Will it be the God of Abraham, Issac, and Jacob that led us.
As for me and my house, we will serve the Lord.
The same thing is going on in the United States of America.
Foreign influences has got us to worship the gods of the world.
America pray for unity in our churches to lead the people to God.
Jesus is the way to glory; accept Him as your Lord and Savior.

William T. Smith

Accept Myself

The curious paradox is that when I accept myself,
Just as I am, then I can change. Carl Rogers.
That is all that Jesus wants out of you and I.
Come unto me as you are, and I will change you.
When I accept the fact that I am a sinner, living in sin.
When I know I need someone to cleanse me from sin.
When I go to Jesus in faith believing that he will accept me.
That is when Jesus will forgive me and accept me as his.
I accept Jesus' gift of salvation, he becomes my advocate.
And Jesus accepts me into his Kingdom, that is His glory.
The work I do here on earth, will be accepted by Father God.
When I meet Jesus face to face, he will accept me into heaven.

William T. Smith

Love

Every time you smile at someone, it is an action of love.

A gift to that person, a beautiful thing. Mother Teresa.

What is love? Unselfish loyal and benevolent concern.

You have this kind of love; you will help a stranger in need.

This is the love Jesus had, when he went to the cross for you.

When we love God, we will want to keep his commandments.

I wish to dwell in the house of my Lord, on earth and in glory.

I wish to see his beauty and to enquire in his temple forever.

I may have trouble here on earth, but Jesus works it for his glory.

And when this trouble comes; I have the Holy Spirit to intercede.

Heavenly Father himself loves you, when you love Christ Jesus.

Jesus came from the Father, and he returned back to the Father.

If you confess Jesus as your Savior here on earth, you show love.

Behold, Jesus stands at your hearts door and knock, let him in.

If you confess Jesus with your mouth and believe in your heart.

Your heart believes unto righteousness, confession unto salvation.

William T. Smith

Doubt-Self Glorification

The worse enemy to creativity is self doubt. Sylvia Plath.

I say the worse enemy to Christianity is self glorification.

When we doubt we lack confidence in ourself or someone.

This lack of confidence will most likely lead to distrust.

Lack of confidence also will make your decisions uncertain.

When you are uncertain about something, you will hesitate.

All of this doubt will make you question yourself and others.

None of which is helpful when you need to make a decision.

We do this same thing in self- glorification of our being.

We give the praise, honor, and worship unto ourselves.

That will lead to an unthankful heart, unto Lord Jesus.

That is when we say our prosperity comes from your hard work.

But the Bible says that God made everything that was made.

When you do not believe that, then you are hurting yourself.

When people see you in that kind of glorification of, self.

It also hurts Christianity, which is a sin against Christ Jesus.

William T. Smith

Laughter

Laughing at our mistakes can lengthen our own life.
Laughing at someone's else's can shorten it. Callen Hightower.
When you laugh are you showing mirth- mercy- joy- or scorn.
You do this with a smile and chuckle or an explosive sound.
Every time you smile it is beautiful; and will up-lift someone.
Which is better than laughing at someone, to bring evil scorn.
Depending on how you laugh at or with someone, tells it all.
When you laugh; enjoying someones mistake, could be dangerous.
When you laugh with someones mistake, could bring inspiration.
If something is amusing, then it will not be taken as ridicule.

William T. Smith

Being Gifted

We must believe that we are gifted for something. Marie Carie.

No matter who you are, you do have a gift, you are gifted.

God made man all different, and gave each one a gift, their very own.

The problem with most people is that they don't want theirs.

You are a gift to someone around you, by what you are doing.

It may be something simple, that you don't think about, but do always.

But that simple act does more for a person than anything else could.

And that in it's self is a gift more people needs to look for in yourself.

But instead; they think they should be a singer or famous lawyer;

Your talent is your gift; not being a comedian or even a movie actor.

Be yourself, do what is good for you and other people is a gift.

And with that you will find your talent and your special gift.

You will know your gift or talent when you do it for Lord Jesus;

When you do it for self-worship, you may miss out on your talent.

William T. Smith

A Soldier

There once was a soldier that proclaimed: "There is no God!".
As he worked and lived a long life on this earthly sod.
Then there came a day, where he came upon this awful sight.
And he proclaimed; would this be God in all of his might.
The soldier looked puzzled and did not know what to say.
This is the tomb, where Jesus' body now does lay?
He looked into the grave and seen nothing but grave cloths.
As he went out he was heard to say; "My boss will not like this".
He knew that death was his that day, and probably die on a cross.
He was guarding the grave of Jesus; and the body gone, was lost.
This soldier was worried and scared; but not like in a fight.
Jesus appeared unto him and said; fear not, I am Jesus the Light.
The soldier said: "Yes! I do believe there is a Living God now".
As he prayed to Jesus for forgiveness; To the ground he bowed.
Jesus gave that soldier peace, joy with salvation that blessed day.
The soldier became a minister and proclaimed Jesus; they say.

William T. Smith

Walk in His Counsel

The Lord has showed you, O man, that you are, what is good.

What does the Lord require of you, but to do justice.

To have and love mercy, and to walk humbly with God.

You do this, then you will stand and feed in His strength.

You shall be a person of peace, with wisdom to understand.

When the Lord becomes your King- Savior and redeemer.

That is when you start to really live a good, honest life.

But woe unto me, for I have never walked in His counsel.

I have put my trust in friends and not this Lord; Christ Jesus.

I know what is good, but do not have the desire for it.

So: What is going to happen to me at the end of my life.

God will give you up to your vile affections and depart from you.

When you stand before the Heavenly Father, you are without excuse.

He will say: "Depart form me you doer of evil" and throw you in hell.

William T. Smith

Angels - Good or Bad

There are angels everywhere on this planet called earth.

All the angels were created for the service unto the Lord.

But something happened at the creation of heaven and earth.

Lucifer an Archangel was in charge of the Mercy Seat of God.

But Lucifer did not want to be in charge of this Mercy Seat.

Lucifer wanted to sit on the Mercy Seat, and be higher than God.

So: Lucifer talked to some of the angels into a rebellion.

This rebellion caused these angels to fall from God's grace.

These are now called demons, evil spirits, or imps of the Devil.

The angels that did not follow Lucifer, in known as good angels.

These angels are messengers unto God the Holy Heavenly Father.

A lot of times they are called guardian or protecting angels.

We are assigned angels to help us to stay safe on the earth.

But: they can not help if our will gets in their way to protect.

William T. Smith

Center Of Salvation

The center of salvation is forgiveness.
Where forgiveness ends, is where love begins.
You cannot have love until you have forgiveness.
Forgiveness for hate, malice, hurts and trespasses.
Once you start to forgive, Jesus starts to heal.
In the middle of the Lord's prayer in Matthew 6:12.
And forgive us our debts, as we forgive our debtors.
And again in Matthew 6:14&15, reads like this:
For if you forgive men their trespasses, (forgive debtors).
Your heavenly Father will also forgive you. (your debts).
But if you forgive not men their trespasses, (sin against you).
Neither will your Father forgive your trespasses. (your sin).
Jesus also said to love others as I have loved you.
Again; the center of salvation is forgiveness of others.
What we forgive, turns into love with your salvation.
You cannot love with bitterness and hate in your soul.
You cannot forgive with bitterness and hate in your soul.
Salvation starts when you ask Jesus to forgive you your sin.
Salvation ends when you are forgiven of all your sin.
That is when we start to live in the love of Christ Jesus.
The love of Christ is to forgive, for they know not what they do.

William T. Smith

Highway To Heaven

You won't find it on a map, but a highway to heaven does exist. "The Roman Road" is explained in the Bible, and it tells how to go to heaven.

We need God's power because we have a problem with sin. "For all have sinned and fall short of the glory of God" (Romans 3:23). "Sin" means missing the mark or missing God's intended destination for us.

None of us can reach that destination on his or her own because everyone is a sinner.

When we work, we earn money. Sin earns wages as well-- wages of death. Because God loves all sinners, He has provided another route: "For the wages of sin is death, but the gift of God is eternal life in Christ Jesus our Lord" (Romans 6:23).

The highway to heaven is found in Romans 10:9: "If you confess with your mouth, "Jesus is Lord", and believe in your heart that God raised Him from the dead, you will be saved." We need to confess our sin and ask God for forgiveness. To confess Jesus as Lord involves agreeing with God about your sin and your need for salvation. You must repent of your sin, turning away from the direction in life which you are going, To "believe in your heart" is to place your faith in Jesus, trusting that He died on a cross for your sins. "But God proves His own love for us in that while we were still sinners Christ died for us." (Romans 5:8).

If you would like to have salvation in Jesus Christ, sincerely pray a prayer like this one, being honest in your heart and believing that Jesus is God's only Son: "Dear God, I confess to You my sin and need for salvation. I turn away from my sin and place my faith in Jesus as my Savior and Lord.

Amen.

Share your faith in Jesus with a Christian friend or pastor. Becoming a Christian is your first step on the lifelong road of spiritual growth and service God desires for you. Follow Christ in believer's baptism by immersion and join a local church.

A Gospel Worker

My version of John 3:14-21

And as Moses lifted up the serpent in the wilderness, even so must Jesus the Son of man be lifted up: That whosoever believes in Jesus should not perish, but have eternal life.

For God so loved mankind, that he gave his only begotten Son, that whosoever believes in Jesus should not perish, but have everlasting life. For God sent not his Son (Jesus) into the world to condemn mankind: but that mankind through him might be saved.

He that believes on Jesus is not condemned: but he that believes not is condemned already, because he did not believe in the name of the only begotten Son of God. And this is the condemnation, that light is come into the world, and mankind loved darkness rather than light, because their deeds were evil. For everyone that does evil hates the light, neither comes to the light, lest his deeds should be reproved, or corrected.

But he that does truth comes to the light, that his deeds may be made manifest, that they are wrought or fashioned in God.

In him (Jesus) was life; and the life was the light of men. John 1:4.

After reading this you may want to go back and read the Highway to Heaven again, with Jesus; the light; being on your mind.

BOOK TEN

Wisdom of God

The reverence of the Lord is the beginning of wisdom.

And the knowledge of the holy is understanding God.

If you lack wisdom, ask God that gives to you liberally.

Ask in faith, wavering not, and wisdom shall be given.

Knowing this, trying of your faith will work patience.

Give thanks unto God for His unspeakable gift of wisdom.

Whosoever believes on Jesus shall not be ashamed of Him.

For whosoever calls upon the name of the Lord shall be saved.

With this; the Spirit of God bears witness with our spirit.

And whosoever is led by the Spirit, are called, sons of God.

The wisdom of God is my strength, my salvation in the storm.

The wisdom of God knows my heart, and knows my thoughts.

I Ask Jesus to search me for any wickedness that is in me.

Remove that from my thought and lead me in the way of everlasting.

William T. Smith

Inspiration to Write

I need an inspiration to write a thought I have.
So I pray to the heavenly Father to help me in this.
The heavenly Father sends to me the Holy Spirit.
The Holy Spirit gives me the unction to write.
I write about what is in God's Word the Bible.
And all that I write must glorify my Lord; Jesus.
Sometimes it may be about friends or family.
At times it may be a funny short story of some sort.
But the inspiration comes from the Holy Spirit.
I do my best to put to words that you can understand.

William T. Smith

What Has The Lord Done For Me?

Question: What has the Lord done for me?

I must think about this; so that I will see.

1st: He has given me life so I can live on earth.

2nd: He has given me love so I can love others.

3rd: He has given me this planet to live on.

4th: He made it possible to grow plants to eat.

5th: He has given me oxygen to breathe while here.

6th: He has given me water to drink and to wash.

7th: He has given me animals to enjoy and to eat.

8th: He has given me a place of shelter to be safe.

9th: He has made it possible to have modern conveniences.

10th: He has made it possible to put clothes on my body.

11th: He has given me this planet with many views to see.

12th: He has given me a body that will heal itself.

13th: He has given me doctors to help with that healing.

14th: He has given me a family to love and be with.

15th: He has given me nature to enjoy with hunting.

16th: He has given me that same nature to camp and fish.

17th: He has given me emotions for different feelings.

18th: Look at the trees He has put on this earth for me.

19th: Trees for shade; trees for fruit; trees to build.

20th: He has put a sun to warm me; and a moon for light.

21st: He has given me His Son Jesus for my salvation.

22nd: He put strips on His Son Jesus for my healing.

23rd: He put a crown of thorns on Jesus for my peace.

24th: He has given me His Holy Spirit for my comfort.

25th: He has given me life after my death here on earth.

26th: A better question is: What hasn't He done for me?

27th: What he has not done was turn His back on me.

28th: What he has not done was let me burn in hells fire.

29th: What he has not done was leave me alone to go my way.

30th: What he has not done was to denied me before His Father.

31st: He has done everything I can think of and much more.

32nd: It's not what the Lord done for me; What have you done for Him?

William T. Smith

Daughters Weep Not

And there followed him a great company of people.

And the women which bewailed and lamented him.

But Jesus turning unto them said, Daughters weep not for me.

But weep for yourselves, and for your children's children.

For behold the day is coming: In which they shall say-

Blessed are the barren: The womb that never bares-

And the babies that do not feed: that are never born unto you.

For they will call out to the mountains to fall on them.

They will want the hills to cover them up for that day.

If you do these things while there is plenty around.

What will you do, when everything drys-up like a desert?

You don't believe in Jesus now, will you believe then?

Jesus told these women what will happen in the future.

Look around and see if not this coming to pass now.

Abortions by the millions every year around the world.

Those who is not aborted, are thrown into trash cans.

William T. Smith
Luke 23:27-32.

Hearken Unto Me

Hear my instruction, and be wise, do not refuse it.

So hearken unto me; all you children of the cross.

For blessed is the person that hears the ways of the Lord.

Blessed is the person that hears me knocking at their door.

For those who finds Jesus finds life, and favor with the Father.

But the one who sins; wrongs his own soul unto death.

A wise man will accept Jesus as Savior and King in their life.

A foolish man will say; I can get into heaven by my works.

So reverence the Lord God Jesus with all your heart and soul.

Be in the counsel of Jesus and learn His ways and peace.

So child of the Cross, pray for yourself, then for your neighbor.

In this you have hearkened unto Jesus and kept his commandments.

William T. Smith

Be Like God

Man was created in the image of God for fellowship.

Man was put in the garden of Eden to take care of it.

God communed with man in the cool of the evening.

It seemed man was very content, but he wanted more.

Lucifer call Serpent went to temp man in this garden.

Man was convinced he should be like God in life.

Man disobeyed God and ate the fruit in the gardens mist.

God told man not to eat for it would bring about death.

First man disobeyed God; now all men must die physically.

Lucifer wanted to be higher than God; man wants to be God.

We go about doing our own thing and leaving God out.

But Jesus came to redeem the sin of disobedience to God.

Jesus paid the price for our disobedience to a living God.

We must all die physically, but not all must die spiritually.

We accept Jesus, we accept his forgiveness for disobeying.

When we accept Jesus; we have communication with God.

We have the fellowship with God like he wanted at first.

We will have eternal life; through the blood of Jesus the Son.

William T. Smith

Never Know

You will never know-
How high you can go-
Until you have seen-
How low you have been-
I have been with the Devil-
And caused a lot of evil-
Until I finally knew this low-
I didn't appreciate Him so-
Once you appreciate Christ Jesus-
Know for sure He took your sinful lust-
You then will go even higher than-
You ever thought you could have been-
All the way into God's glorious heaven-
Where you will be in eternity with Him.

William T. Smith

Will We All Get Into Heaven?

There is a song that goes; When we all get to heaven.
What a day of rejoicing that will be, when we see Jesus.
The fact is; we all will not go to heaven, some will go to hades.
But: we will all see Jesus, and His nail scared hands.
Those of us that received Jesus as LORD and King.
Will enter into heaven, where we will have perfect rest.
But: for those who denied Jesus as their Lord and King.
Will be judged and told to depart from him into torment.
They will go into the Lake of Fire, made for Satan and his angels.
For their father is Lucifer- My Father is God Almighty.

William T. Smith

When I Get To Heaven

We worry about money; What is bought and sold.
When I get to heaven; I will walk on pure gold.
We worry about getting things done in the day time.
When I get to heaven; No worries- Jesus is the Son shine.
We never have time to sit and visit with friends and family.
When I get to heaven; I will talk with everyone for eternity.
We worry about what we eat, and drink, and what to wear.
When I get to heaven; Jesus has a table spread, and clothes there.
We worry a lot about getting old and helpless and death.
When I get to heaven; I will never grow old, nor will I die.

William T. Smith

My Privilege

It is not just a right we have to believe in Jesus;
But it is a privilege to believe in a Savior, Jesus.
Demons believes in Jesus, and they tremble of it.
I believe in Jesus, the Son and made Him my Lord.
Jesus is God Creator, came to earth as a human.
To me He is God, my Savior and my Redeemer.
I asked Jesus to forgive me of all my sinful ways.
I ask the Father in Jesus' name, my Lord may say yes.
As long as it is something that will not harm me.
He may say no! Because it may lead to me sinning.
Sin will harm me in many ways, I will lose relationship.
So I do trust Jesus in all that I do and say every day.
Sin keeps me out of fellowship and out of his kingdom.
I will trust Jesus with my heart, my soul, my life I win.
That is much more than a right to believe in Jesus.
It is a privilege to believe, and receive eternal life.

William T. Smith

Complain

What happens when you complain about what life brought?
It brings strife upon you, and you end up with a harden heart.
We then look around to see who or what we can put the blame.
It will be anybody else, or it may be any thing handy; not me.
We are human; human nature does not like to take responsibility.
Because the things we are saying or doing, causes the problem.
In stead of taking the blame, It will always be someone's fault.
We are under a curse; and the curse will come back on ourself.
The curse came by and through Lucifer; the Devil, the evil one.
Who will always block the Light from God, and Jesus the Son.
Jesus will always bring His Light to the center of the problem.
When we take responsibility for our action, it keeps us from sin.
Never complain about a situation, Just give it to the Lord God.
God made us, and knows how to handle what goes on in life.

William T. Smith

Wisdom of God

The reverence of the Lord is the beginning of wisdom.

And the knowledge of the holy is understanding God.

If you lack wisdom, ask God that gives to you liberally.

Ask in faith, wavering not, and wisdom shall be given.

Knowing this, trying of your faith will work patience.

Give thanks unto God for His unspeakable gift of wisdom.

Whosoever believes on Jesus shall not be ashamed of Him.

For whosoever calls upon the name of the Lord shall be saved.

With this; the Spirit of God bears witness with our spirit.

And whosoever is led by the Spirit, are called, sons of God.

The wisdom of God is my strength, my salvation in the storm.

The wisdom of God knows my heart, and knows my thoughts.

I Ask Jesus to search me for any wickedness that is in me.

Remove that from my thought and lead me in the way of everlasting.

William T. Smith

Conceited

Being conceited is having an excessively high opinion of yourself.

What you are: is being so proud of yourself, you will not listen.

For all that is in the world; lust of the flesh, and lust of the eyes.

As well as the pride of life, that is of your father, Lucifer and world.

And whosoever is a friend of the world, is an enemy of Creator God.

Do not be a novice: a beginner and not having the experience needed.

Being this way will lead to pride; and conceit is knocking at the door.

This lets Satan in and you fall into condemnation of the Devil's trap.

And God hates evil ways: pride, arrogance and a froward mouth.

For out of the mouth of a fool comes pride, conceit and arrogance.

Woe to the crown of pride, and drunkards who think they are strong.

Your terribleness has deceived you with the pride of your heart.

Lord: hide me from the presence of the prideful lust of an evil man.

Let me reverence the Lord with His knowledge and understanding.

To be carnally minded is death; The carnal mind is an enemy to God.

To be spiritual minded is life and peace; which leads to eternal Life.

William T. Smith

BOOK ELEVEN

Imagination

A person without imagination is like a teabag without hot water.
All though this is a very good quote by Alan Fletcher.
I think I should change it just a little bit, to get imagination rolling.
A person without Jesus is like a teabag without hot water, dried-up.
Without imagination you will live a hum drum life here on earth.
Without Jesus you will live a life in disobedient to Father God.
You can have imagination without Jesus in your life as Savior.
But you cannot have Jesus in your life, and not have imagination.
You can have faith and have it abundantly without Jesus in your life.
You cannot have Jesus in your life without faith of a mustard seed.
I believe it is better to have Jesus in my life with imagination; than:
To have the whole world at my fingertip, with worldly imagination.
With Jesus, his faith, his imagination, I have total peace, joy and life.
With the world and its faith, its imagination, all you get is chaos.

William T. Smith

Patience

Knowing this, that the trying of your faith works patience. James 1:3.

But let patience have her perfect work manifested (in your life).

That you may be perfect in your spirit, wanting nothing (worldly).

And if you lack wisdom, ask God who will give it to you (abundantly).

For God gives wisdom liberally to all that ask him (in faith believing).

Ask in faith, with nothing wavering, and you will receive. James 1:4-5.

I wait for the lord, my soul does wait, and in his word I hope. Psalms 130:5.

So I wait for his mercy, the one that made all things possible on earth.

Give your ear, and wait and keep silent for God's counsel will come.

Be not ashamed to wait on the LORD, he will answer in due time.

Lord let my prayer be unto you at an acceptable time and season.

That your mercy will give me the patience I need, in order to wait.

For those that wait upon the Lord shall renew their strength. Isaiah 40:41.

For the Lord faints not, neither does he get weary in his power.

Patience is a virtue for those who wait, before they get angry and mean.

A little patience can go a lot farther than malice and what comes after.

William T. Smith

Anxious

Anxious is characterized by, and resulting from worry.
It is also a painful or apprehensive uneasiness of mind.
So the Lord said: "Do not be anxious about anything;
But in every situation, by prayer and petition present;
With thanksgiving present your request to God".
For he who is Almighty, the one who brings all things;
Together for good, is the one who will meet your needs.
Because: if God is for us, who then can be against us?
So pray without ceasing, and in everything give thanks;
For this is the will of God in Christ Jesus our Lord.
Worry only causes problems with family, God and body.
What profits a person who is always worrying about that.

William T. Smith

Reprobate Mind

And even as they did not like to retain God's knowledge.

God gave them over to a reprobate mind for things unnatural.

That is people wanting to do ungodly acts against, Almighty.

Doing things that are not convenient in mind or in the body.

Then he will reject them as unworthy for righteousness.

Wherefore God will give them up to the uncleanness of lust.

They will dishonor their bodies, between themselves freely.

Homosexuality and fornication is every where you look.

When a person becomes so corrupt in their ways and deals;

Then that person is unacceptable for Jesus to use in his work.

In whose eyes is a vile person condemned in what he is doing.

Jesus knows the heart of a vile man and his ways are condemned.

When you go against God's law and disobey the truth in word.

Then you are a reprobate in what you do and in all you say.

Jesus is the only way unto salvation of this evil vile living.

Accept him as your Savior and he will cleanse your heart.

William T. Smith

Reality And Dreams

Reality and dreams are everywhere, Just look around you.

That is true and clear, where ever you look, it is real indeed.

So reality is: How you live on this planet called earth.

So Dreams is: How you want to live on this planet called earth.

But: Your reality and your dreams can work together for you.

The reality you want is the dream of peace and joy in your life.

Go to Jesus; believing he is God in the flesh, who died for you.

He is willing to give you peace and joy with salvation of soul.

Then the way you live your life after that will show love in all.

Your dream now will be the dream you want; peace and joy.

Without Jesus it is only a dream that may never come true.

With Jesus it is a reality, and Jesus gives peace joy with love.

William T. Smith

Evil or the Lord

The Lord brought Israel out of Egypt from a 400 year bondage.

The Lord said: "you shall not have any other gods before you".

The Lord said to Jonah; Go to Nineveh and speak against them.

Nineveh had become a wicked and perverse place on earth.

The people shall turn to me, you preach my truth I have given you.

The sin of Sodom and Gomorrah is great and very grievous.

The people has turned away their ears from the truth of the Lord.

He that sins against the Lord, wrongs his own soul unto death.

The eyes of mankind is never satisfied in their destruction of self.

These things are written, so that you will know this evil that lures.

This I am writing so you may believe in the Lord Jesus, God's Son.

The Lord has showed you what is good and righteous, in his word.

And what does the Lord require of you, but to do justly with others.

Show mercy to others, and to walk humbly with your God; Jesus.

In all things, ask in prayer believing that you will receive from him.

Jesus said: "I am the resurrection, and the life believe in me".

The body is dead because of sin; The Spirit gives life eternal.

As many that are led by the Spirit of God, through Christ Jesus.

They shall inherit eternal life to be called sons of God Almighty.

William T. Smith

Vain Words

No matter who you are; or what you have done in this life;
You will appear before the judgment seat of Christ Jesus.
There you will receive the things done with your body.
It makes no difference if it was good things or bad things.
Let no person deceive you with their vain words of wisdom.
You walked in darkness, just like they are walking in darkness.
You came to the knowledge of the Light you have in the Lord.
So therefore walk in the light, as children of the Light of Jesus.
For a good man will bring forth good treasure from his heart.
An evil man will bring forth evil treasure from lust of the world.
So above all things put on love, which is the bond of perfection.
Have peace of God in your heart, so that it may rule your body.
For the fruit of the Spirit is in all goodness and righteousness.
Proving what is acceptable unto the Lord in what you say and do.

William T. Smith
Taken from: Matthew 12; II Corinthians 5;
Ephesians 5; and Colossians 3.

Thoughts Of God

The Lord said that he knows the thoughts he has toward you.

Thoughts are of peace, not of evil, to receive an expected end.

The Lord can do anything, and no thought is withheld from him.

The Lord knows the thoughts of mankind, and they are empty.

The thoughts of the Lord, are not your thoughts O mortal man

Neither are mankind's earthly ways, the same as the Lord's ways.

As you know the heavens are higher than the earth;

So God's ways and thoughts are higher than man's ways and thoughts.

The Lord knows all the thoughts of a wise person and calls it vain.

Let no man deceive himself; thinking he is wise in the world.

For the man that thinks himself to be wise, becomes a fool.

For the wisdom of the world is foolishness with God Almighty.

I know nothing of myself here on earth in the things I say and do.

But what I do for my Lord is justified, because he called me for that.

How precious also are your thoughts unto me, O Lord God.

How great is the sum of them; they are more in number than I can count.

William T. Smith
Taken from: Jeremiah 29;
Job 42; Psalms 94 & 139; Isaiah 55; and I Corinthians 3.

God's Trinity

The LORD by wisdom made the earth, by understanding made the heavens.

By the LORD'S knowledge the water is held back and clouds have rain.

There are three that bear record in heaven; Father, Word, and Holy Spirit.

There are three that bear witness in the earth; spirit, water and blood.

There is one body, one Spirit and one hope, even as you are called.

There is one Lord, one faith and one baptism, which gives grace as a gift.

Now abides faith,hope charity, but the greatest is charity or love.

If I have understanding, and knowledge and faith to move mountains.

But I do not have Love; what good is understanding, knowledge and faith.

Love will never fail, but prophecies, tongues, and knowledge surely will.

I am the LORD, your Holy One, your Creator, and your King your Savior.

There is One God and Father of all, and above all,

and through all, and in all.

Jesus said I will go away and I will send another to be your comforter.

He will come to reprove the world of sin, righteousness,and judgment.

Of sin, because the people does not believe on the Lord Jesus, their Savior.

Of righteousness; because I go to the Father, and not be here in flesh.

Of judgment, because the prince of this world (Satan) is judged already.

I write all these things so that you may believe on the One Christ Jesus.

William T. Smith

Thank You Lord Jesus

Come and hear all you that reverence the Lord God.
I will declare what he has done for my sinful soul.
My- my how my soul is troubled, and I do fear death.
Lord; Jesus save me from this troubled sin that I have.
Jesus answered me and said: Keep my commandments.
Keep your heart pure with understanding of my Word.
In whatever you do, always give thanks to Christ Jesus.
This is the will of the heavenly Father concerning you.
Be careful for nothing; but in everything by prayer.
Rejoice in the Lord always; and again I say; Rejoice.
Hide not your face from me in the day of trouble; Lord.
You forgave all my iniquities; and healed my disease.
Let the peace of God rule in my heart, soul and body.
I know you hear me when I pray with supplications.
The Lord of the heavens bless me and kept me safe.
And I will sing my praise in your name as I rejoice.

William T. Smith

When Born Anew

I am in Christ, with that I am now a new creature with God.

All the old things I have done are now passed away in Jesus.

Behold! All things have become new, sense he reconciled me.

Jesus is the way, the truth, and the life unto redemption.

By man came death, so by man came also the resurrection.

For Adam sinned and all die; Christ came to make all alive.

Jesus told Nicodemus; Except a man be born again he will not live.

You have to be born of water and Spirit to enter the kingdom of God.

For what is born of the flesh stays flesh through out his life time.

What is born of the Spirit, has the Spirit of God living in them.

Seek the Lord now, while he may still be found in your life.

Call upon Jesus now, while he is near for the salvation of the soul.

Jesus said: "You will know the truth, and the truth will set you free".

Study your Bible prayerfully, and pray without ceasing continually.

William T. Smith

Temple of God

Know not that you are the temple of a living God?
And the Spirit of God that dwells in you as holy.
Know you not that your body is the member of Christ?
Your body is for the Lord; and the Lord is for the body.
So what part of the body believes with an infidel's body?
Or what part of the body is in agreement with idols?
Know you not that your body is the temple of the Holy Spirit?
Which is in you, and you with Jesus, and the body is not yours.
You are the body of Christ, and members of his church.
You have many gifts, in which you can glorify the body.
As your body or temple is one, but has many members.
So the church of God is one, but has many members unto God.
The members of your body works together as a single unit.
The members of the church works together as a single unit.
Therefore do not criticize your fellow member by denomination.
But rejoice in the Lord all members of the Lord Jesus Christ.

William T. Smith

BOOK TWELVE

Mercy Seat

God has highly exalted Jesus, and gave him a name above all names.
That the name of Jesus every knee should bow in heaven and earth.
And that every tongue should confess that Jesus is Lord God.
After the Lord had spoken to the disciples he departed to heaven.
There he is seated on the right hand of the Father on the Mercy Seat.
In his presence is joy, at the right hand there are pleasures evermore.
Seek not after your own heart and let your eyes go about whoring.
But seek the righteousness of Jesus, and let your heart be of him.
You shall see the Son of man sitting on the right side of power.
You shall also see the Son of man coming in the clouds of heaven.
Behold, Jesus is coming quickly: with rewards for mankind.
He will give every man according to his work, it shall be known.

William T. Smith

Lord You Are My God

Lord; you are my God, you are the one and only one.
You sent your Son (Jesus) to a cross, to die for me.
Jesus is my Savior, my God, my Creator, my all in all.
Jesus' blood cleanest me from all my unrighteousness.
Jesus is the one; yes: He is the only one that I pray to.
You cannot have salvation, until Jesus you accepted.
Jesus was there when heaven and earth was created.
Jesus was there when I was brought into this world.
The Spirit of Jesus dwells in my heart and soul today.
For it was Jesus' blood that washed my sin all away.
Now Jesus lives in me and he gives me peace within.
With that peace, I must honor my Lord in living right.
And when I die, I will not have a second death in hell.
Because; I had my second birth, when I accepted Jesus.
I will have a home in glory, like my Savior promised.
And will live through-out eternity with my Lord; Jesus.

William T. Smith

Jesus Died; What Happened?

When Jesus received the vinegar he gave up the ghost.

Jesus cried with a load voice, when he gave up the ghost.

The centurion seen what was done and gloried God.

The centurion said: Certainly this was a righteous man.

The veil of the temple was torn from top to bottom.

For God tore the veil at the top, so we would believe.

If it was torn from the bottom, it would appear man did it.

The earth did quake and the rocks rent, or separated, split.

The graves were opened, and dead bodies arose; being alive.

They came out and went into the holy city and appeared to many.

A soldier pierced Jesus' side, to make sure Jesus was dead.

Blood did not flow from the wound, instead it was water.

The soldier seeing this did not break the legs of Jesus.

The centurion saw this and was greatly afraid.

And the centurion declared that Jesus was the Son of God.

Many women were there looking from afar, who followed Jesus.

Evening was here, the preparation, the day before the sabbath.

Joseph a counselor asked for the body of Jesus, to bury him.

The body could not stay on the cross, it was the Sabbath.

This Sabbath day was an high day, or the high Sabbath.

He had to take the body down, for it was the day of preparation.

He wrapped the body in clean linen, and the Sabbath drew on.

In Leviticus, God told Moses to have seven feast or seven holy days.

These holy day would fall on a day before the seventh day sabbath.

Make this a holy convocation- even the feast of the passover.

The next day will be the feast of unleavened bread- a holy day.

The next day following the day of preparation- a holy day.

The chief Priests remembered Jesus saying in the temple;

That deceiver said, After three days, I will rise again.

They sent soldiers to seal the tomb and to keep watch.

On the first day of the week, Mary came to prepare the body.

The tomb was open and nothing but the clean linen was there.

Jesus AROSE from the grave; just as he said he would.

To be a Christian is to believe what was written in the Bible.

Read Matthew 27:50- ; Mark 15:37- ; Luke 23:46- ; John 19:30- .

For the holy days read; Leviticus 23; and Deuteronomy 15;.

Do not harden your heart, and not believe that Jesus arose.

The cry will be unto the Lord against you, and it will be a sin.

William T. Smith

Mercy Endures

O give thanks unto the Lord; because he is good.
O give thanks unto the Lord; for his mercy endures.
O sing your praises unto the Lord with instruments.
For he is good; and his mercy endures forever and ever.
Sing together; give thanks unto the Lord, for he is good.
His mercy endures forever, towards those who love him.
Praise you the Lord, O give thanks unto the Lord.
For he is good: for his mercy endures forever and ever.
Let the redeemed of the Lord say so about his mercy.
Let all the people of the Lord say; his mercy is forever.
O give thanks unto the Lord of lords; and God of gods.
He brought you out of sin with a strong hand and arm.
Again there shall be heard in this place that I inhabitant.
The voice of joy, and the voice of gladness being raised.
The voice of the Bridegroom, and the voice of the Bride.
And the voice of them that say; Praise the Lord of hosts.
For his mercy endures forever, where salvation is given.
What you deserve is torment; Jesus gives you peace and joy.

William T. Smith

Pray To God

There is nothing so big that God cannot handle it.

There is nothing so little that God will put it aside.

When you pray, find a time that you can be alone.

Remove anything that may distract you from praying.

God is where ever you are, he wants you to be focused.

The phone rings, let it ring, if important there is a message.

When you pray, have an agenda in place that is pacific.

Do not have a random prayer, as you would during the day.

As Jesus prayed for things, he also prayed not for the world.

Meaning: he wanted his followers to be safe to do his work.

The Lord has a plan for your life, to help you not hurt you.

Sometimes something will happen, that will cause hurt.

Always remember that Jesus will help you through the hurt.

He may not take the hurt away, as a reminder for you to pray.

If it is something that concerns you, it concerns the Lord.

If it is something you are going through, Jesus wants to help.

But stay focused, be in a quiet place and pray earnestly.

Jesus wants a relationship with you, not just a worker.

William T. Smith

Insurance's

The people of today has all kinds of insurance.

They have Auto insurance, in case of an accident.

They have Service insurance, in case of a break-down.

They have Home insurance, in case of damaged home.

They have Health insurance, in case of bad health.

They have Medicare insurance, to help pay the bill.

They have Life insurance, so your children can live good.

They have Burial insurance, to help pay the funeral.

They have Crop insurance, in case the farmer's crop is bad.

For everything that we have, there is an insurance policy.

But: what about your soul, do you have a policy for your soul.

There is one out there, and it seems nobody wants it.

This insurance is the most important insurance you can have.

The insurance of eternal life in glory with Christ Jesus.

The cost of this insurance is believing Jesus, is God.

That Jesus came into this world to bring salvation to us.

That Jesus died on the cross to pay for your redemption.

With all that, He takes your sin, and gives you peace and joy.

The best insurance you can have is through the blood of Jesus.

William T. Smith

Believe

We all believe in things, and some of the things are false.
We will believe a lie, before we believe the truth about it.
There are myths out there that was started with no substance.
We believe myths without ever thinking how they originated.
Some of them we believe are called "Old wise tells", stories.
Some may have started to keep your child from something bad.
Like eating fruit skins, or a lie will make your nose grow big.
Or telling them something, to keep them from going someplace.
Now we have movies that is nothing more than a written story.
But because we see the stunts made in the movie, we believe it.
But not all the things we believe are lies; some are indeed true.
The Bible is written on the truth about the people of that time.
And is relevant in this day and age we are living in now.
The Bible is full of truths about many different subjects
This is God's word, given to mankind as a gift unto righteousness.
Jesus is the Son of the Holy Father, living in the flesh of man.
Jesus is God, Jesus is man, Jesus knows heavenly and earthly things.
Man sinned against Creator God, and death is the punishment.
Jesus came to earth to redeem mankind from that punishment.
He done this by dying on a cross, after being falsely accused.
This is hard to believe, because of all our unbelief of Jesus.
But when we say yes to Jesus, we experience a holy peace.

William T. Smith

Respected and Idolized

Everyone should be respected as an individual,
But: no one should be idolized. Albert Einstein.
They were offended in him, but Jesus said unto them.
A prophet is not without honor, save in his own country;
And in his own house: Christ Jesus. Matthew 13:57.
All gods of the nation are idols; Worship God Almighty.
God should be respected for he made heaven and earth.
God should be idolized because his mercy forgives.
Jesus should be respected for he died on the cross for us.
Jesus should be idolized for he did not stay in the grave.
Respect Jesus because he takes a dead soul living in sin.
And gives that soul a purpose, and eternal life with him.
Idolize Jesus because he is God in earthly form, to redeem.
He redeems us from a life of sin; and gives peace within.
No one on earth should be an idol, but many are idolized.
You should respect everyone; for all humans are God's.
You will live with him forever in heaven, or glory eternally.
Or; you will die without him in hell or torment eternally.

William T. Smith

Father of Lights

Thank you Father for all the lights you have given earth.

The light of the sun, and the light of the moon, and stars.

God said: Let there be lights in the firmament of heaven.

Let these lights divide the day from the night. Genesis 1:14.

Let these lights be for signs, for seasons, and for years.

God made two great lights, one for day the other for night.

The lights was put in there place to divide light from dark.

When God was finished, he looked it over and said it was good.

And this was the fourth day of creation. Genesis 1:14-19.

But before he made these lights, he made another light for earth.

God created heaven and earth, and darkness was upon the deep.

God said let there be light: and behold there was light.

When God saw this light he said was good, Day and Night.

In the beginning was the Word, and the Word was with God.

All things were made by him; in him was life, the life is light.

This light shined in the darkness; and the darkness knew it not.

Jesus is the true Light, which lights every human in the world.

When you receive the Light of Jesus; which is the Word of God.

Then he gives you power to become sons of God, after you believe.

Jesus gives grace and truth, to the one that accepts salvation.

You must confess and deny not that Jesus is the Light of God.

William T. Smith

Seven Things The Lord Hates

These six things does the Lord hate: yea seven are an abomination unto him.

A proud look, a lying tongue, and hands that shed innocent blood.

An heart that devises wicked imaginations, feet that be swift in running to mischief.

A false witness that speaks lies, and he that sows discord among brethren.

1. A proud look: Arrogant, haughty, over bearing look, pride in yourself.

   He is proud, knowing nothing, but envy and strife. I Timothy 6:4.

2. A lying tongue: marked by giving falsehood, being dishonest, not trustworthy.

   Put away lying, neither give a place to the Devil. Ephesians 4:25.

3. Shed innocent blood: free from guilt or sin, harmless, blameless.

   In your skirts is found the blood of innocent souls. Jeremiah 2:34.

4. Heart that devises wicked imaginations: to plan or bring about, invent, plot.

   You devise wicked devises to destroy the people with lying words. Isaiah 32:7.

5. Feet swift to run to mischief: a cause or source of harm, evil, mischievous.

They speak peace with neighbors, but have mischief in their heart. Psalms 28:3.

6. A false witness: not genuine, misleading, untrue, deceive, wrong, lies.

   Do not raise a false report, and be a wicked, unrighteous witness. Exodus 23:1.

7. Sows discord: lack of agreement, disagree, strife, conflict, trouble maker.

   A man that sows discord among brethren, is a false witness and a lier. Proverbs 6:19.

There is away that seems right unto a man, but the end there of are the ways of death.

Forgiveness does not change the past, but it does enlarge the future. Paul Lewis Boese.

We can never rewrite what we did in our life, we can write a new beginning with Christ.

William T. Smith

Seven Things The Lord Loves

These six things does the Lord love, yea; seven are a blessing unto him.
A humble look, A truthful tongue, deliver of the oppressed, a clean glad heart,
Feet of them that preach, A true witness, and a peacemaker.

1. A humble look: meek, modest, gentle, enduring patience, not overbearing.

   He that humbles himself, will be exalted with grace. Micah 6:8.

2. A truthful tongue: sincerity in action, character, and utterance.

   Speak you the truth to his neighbor and execute judgment. Psalms 15:2

3. Deliver of the oppressed: to burden spiritually, unjust or cruel authority.

   When seeing one suffer wrongly, defend him from the oppressor. Jeremiah 22:3.

4. A clean heart: delicate, generally pleasant, fair, spiritually pure.

   Create in me a clean heart, and renew a right spirit in me. Psalms 51:10.

5. Feet that preach: to proclaim publicly, to bring the gospel, to exhort.

   How beautiful are the feet of the one that preach the gospel of peace. Romans 10:15.

6. A true witness: faithful, steadfast, loyal, honest, just, and legitimate.

A true witness delivers souls; so be you true and faithful. Psalms 15:2.

7. A peacemaker: a state of tranquility, state of security, harmony. And the fruit of righteousness is sown in peace to make peace. James 3:18.

Remember the Creator in all that you do, and say, and think;

So that the days of your life will be filled with peace and happiness.

God will bring every work into judgment and all it's secrets.

Be those works be for good or evil, they are judged in truth of God.

William T. Smith

Is Abortion in the Bible?

Abortion as a word, is not in the Bible, but the implication is.

Having an abortion is a monstrosity, or a shocking experience.

For their feet run to evil, and make haste to shed blood.

For your hands are defiled with blood, your fingers with iniquity.

I have sinned in that I have betrayed the innocent blood.

Lord Jesus said; that he hates hands that sheds innocent blood.

Their feet run to evil, and they make haste to shed innocent blood.

Their thoughts are thoughts of iniquity, waiting in destruction.

Remember, I pray, whoever perish, being innocent before life;

That they will come to the grave, and know their seed did not grow!!!

God cannot hear your prayer, when your hands are full of blood.

And they lay and wait for their own blood, for their own lives.

Abortion is in the Bible, it is against man, nature, and God Creator.

Even though you had an abortion or helped in or with an abortion;

You can still get forgiveness if you ask Jesus with an honest heart.

Although your sins be as scarlet, they shall be white as snow.

Although they be like crimson, they shall be as white as wool.

That whosoever believes in Jesus should not parish but have life.

Come unto Jesus with your burden of sin, He will give you rest.

Forgive the trespasses of your fellow person,and be forgiven.

For sin shall not have dominion over you, if you are under grace.

For whosoever shall call upon the name of the Lord shall be saved.

Therefore there is no condemnation to you which are in Christ.

Ask for Jesus to forgive you of your sin as you forgive others.
Then go out and sin no, more, for you have been redeemed.

William T. Smith
This was taken from; Proverbs 1:16, 6:17, 1:18; Job 4:7.
Isaiah 59:3; 59:7; 1:15; Matthew 27:4; 11:28; John 3:15.

Insurance After Death

You have your life insured? That is good.

You have your home or car insured against fire or other damages?

Well enough.

You have insurance to insure the education of your child or children? That's fine.

You have sickness and accident insurance? Good enough.

You may have various other kinds of insurance; but wait! Don't stop with this present life. Go beyond that: insure your life after death. You ask, How? Easy enough, and best of all, it's FREE!

Have the assurance of eternal life. The Word of God says, "All have sinned, and come short of the glory of God"(Romans 3:23)."For the wages of sin is death; but the gift of God is eternal life through Jesus Christ our Lord"Romans 6:23).

Therefore, every one of us should be intensely interested in the question of how to find salvation.

Why will you sell your soul so cheaply?

Why are you neglecting eternity?

Friend, realize your hopeless and helpless condition. Repent. "Believe on the Lord Jesus Christ, and thou shalt be saved"(Acts 16:31)."For God so loved the world, that he gave his only begotten Son, that whosoever believeth in him should not perish, but have everlasting life"(John 3:16).

Study your Bible prayerfully (II Timothy 2:15),and"pray without ceasing' (I Thessalonians 5:17).

And that, my friend, is the way to insure your life after death and to have that blessed assurance of everlasting life.

A Gospel Worker

If we say that we have no sin, we deceive ourselves, and the truth is not in us. If we confess our sins, he is faithful and just to forgive us our sins, and to cleanse us from all unrighteousness. (I John 1:8-9).If you forgive men their trespasses, your heavenly Father will also forgive you: But if you forgive not men their trespasses, neither will your Father forgive your trespasses. (Matthew 6:14-15).

Then spake Jesus again unto them, saying, I am the light of the world: he that follows me shall not walk in darkness, but shall have the light of life.(John 8:12).In him was life; and the life was the light of men. (John 1:5).The Lord is my light and my salvation; whom shall I fear? The LORD is the strength of my life; of whom shall I be afraid.(Psalms 27:1).

Jesus answered, My kingdom is not of this world: if my kingdom were of this world, then would my servants fight, that I should not be delivered to the Jews: but now is my kingdom not from here. Pilate therefore said unto him, Art you a king then? To this end was I born, and for this cause came I into the world, that I should bear witness unto the truth. Every one that is of the truth hears my voice.(John 18:36-37).

For if God spared not the angels that sinned, but cast them down to hell, and delivered them into chains of darkness, to be reserved unto judgment; And spared not the old world, but saved Noah the eighth person, a preacher of righteousness, bringing in the flood upon the world of the ungodly.(II Peter 2: 4-5).What do you think he will do to the unbeliever, and those who reject him of today?

Jesus' Last Prayer

John 16:31 to 17:26

Jesus answered them, Do you now believe? Behold the hour comes, yes, is now come, that you shall be scattered, every man to his own house, and shall leave me alone: and yet I am not alone, because the Father is with me. These things I have spoken unto you, that in me you might have peace.

In the world you shall have tribulation: but be of good cheer; I have overcome the world.

These words spake Jesus, and lifted up his eyes to heaven, and said, Father, the hour is come; glorify your Son, that your Son also may glorify you: As you have given him power over all flesh, that he should give eternal life to as many as you have given him. And this is life eternal, that they might know you the only true God, and Jesus Christ, whom you have sent. I have glorified you on earth: I have finished the work which you gave me to do.

And now, O Father, glorify you in me with your own self with the glory which I had with you before the world was. I have manifested your name unto the men which you gave me out of the world: yours they were, and you gave them to me; and they have kept your word. Now they have known that all things whatsoever you have given me are of you. For I have given unto them the words which you gave me; and they have received them, and have known surely that I came out from you, and they have believed that you did send me.

I pray for them: I pray not for the world, but for them which you have given me; for they are yours. And all mine are yours, and yours are mine; and I am glorified in them. And now I am no more in the world, but these are in the world, and I come to you. Holy Father, keep through your own name those whom you have given me, that they may be one, as we are one.

While I was with them in the world, I kept them in your name: those that you gave me I have kept, and none of them is lost, but the son of perdition (or the son of destruction); that the scripture might be fulfilled. And now come I to you; and these things I speak in the world, that they might have my joy fulfilled in themselves. I have given them your word; and the world have hated them, because they are not of the world, even as I am not of the world.

I pray not that you should take them out of the world, but that you should keep them from the evil of this world. They are not of this world, even as I am not of this world. Sanctify them through your truth: your word is truth. As you have sent me into the world, even so have I also sent them into the world. And for their sakes I sanctify myself, that they also might be sanctified through the truth.

Neither pray I for these alone, but for them also which shall believe on me through their words;

That they all may be one; as you, Father, are in me, and I in you, that they also may be one in us; that the world may believe that you have sent me. And the glory which you gave me I have given them, that they may be one, even as we are one: I in them, and you in me, that they may be made perfect in one; and that the world may know that you have sent me, and have loved them, as you have loved me.

Father, I will that they also, whom you have given me, be with me where I am; that they may behold my glory, which you have given me: for you loved me before the foundation of the world. O righteous Father, the world has not known you: but I have known you, and these have known that you have sent me. And I have declared unto them your name, and will declare it: that the love wherewith you have loved me, may be in them, and I in them.

There is no Amen or anything to close this prayer; for this prayer was left open for Jesus to finish while he was on the cross. When Jesus said "it is finished:" in John 19:30, that ended his earthly prayer for all generations. With that Jesus paid the price for our sin here on earth; all we have to do is ask

Jesus to forgive us for the disobedience to God the Father. Jesus did not finish there, He also breathed on us the Holy Spirit.

In the book of Ecclesiastes 4:8-12, this is what is written: There is one alone, and there is not a second; No, he has neither child or brother: yet is there no end of all his labor; neither is his eye satisfied with riches; neither says he, For whom do I labor, and bereave (deprived) my soul of good?

This is also vanity, Yes, it is sore travail (torture).

Two are better than one; because they have a good reward for their labor. For if they fall, the one will lift up his fellow: but woe to him that is alone when he falls; for he has not another to help him up.

Again, if two lie together, then they have heat: but how can one be warm alone? And if one prevail against him, two shall withstand him; and a threefold cord is not quickly broken.

This is what Jesus was saying in his prayer; the Father is in Jesus; Jesus is in the Christian; the Christian is in the Father as well as in Jesus. That makes me part of a threefold cord, and this cord is not quickly broken.

Jesus did not stop there, no, not by a long shot. When you look into John 20:21-23 Jesus tells us this: Then Jesus said unto them again, Peace be unto you: as my Father has sent me, even so I send you.

And when he had said this, he breathed on them, and said unto them, Receive you the Holy Spirit: Whose soever sins you remit (forgive what they did to you), they are remitted (not holding a grudge) unto them; and whose soever sins you retain (remember), they are retained (held accountable for).

Jesus is telling us to forgive your fellow person just as he has forgiven you; do not hold a grudge or do not hold the person accountable to you for their action. With this the cord he was talking about is not a threefold cord; but now it is a fourfold cord: the Father in Jesus, Jesus in the Christian, the Christian in the Holy Spirit, the Holy Spirit in the Father, The Father, Lord Jesus, Holy Spirit, and the Christian (Child of God). This is a fourfold cord that is impossible to break. Why? God has ordained it to be this way; if not we would be tossed from one side to another.

The way I look at Jesus' last prayer
William T. Smith